What I Say

What I Say

Innovative Poetry by Black Writers in America

EDITED BY ALDON LYNN NIELSEN AND LAURI RAMEY

THE UNIVERSITY OF ALABAMA PRESS
Tuscaloosa

Typeface: Minion and Goudy Sans

Cover illustration: Courtesy of Anna Everett
Cover design: Michele Myatt Quinn

∞

The paper on which this book is printed meets the minimum requirements of American
National Standard for Information Sciences—Permanence of Paper for Printed Library
Materials, ANSI Z39.48–1984.

Library of Congress Cataloging-in-Publication Data

What I say : innovative poetry by black writers in America / edited by Aldon Lynn
Nielsen and Lauri Ramey.
     pages cm. — (Modern and Contemporary Poetics)
    Includes bibliographical references.
    ISBN 978-0-8173-5800-6 (pbk. : alk. paper) — ISBN 978-0-8173-8800-3 (e book)
1. American poetry—African American authors. 2. American poetry—20th century.
3. African Americans—Poetry. 4. Poetics. I. Nielsen, Aldon Lynn, editor. II. Ramey,
Lauri, editor.
  PS591.N4W46 2014
  811'.5080896073—dc23

                                                                          2014021616

In Memoriam

Amiri Baraka

"Fashion this, from the irony of the world."

Contents

Preface

A few words on the collection:

This is the long-planned second volume of the anthology project that began with *Every Goodbye Ain't Gone*. The division between the two collections is chronological, though we have chosen not to announce that explicitly in the titles of the volumes.

The first volume began with writers, such as Russell Atkins and Melvin B. Tolson, who were already engaging in formal experimentation in the 1940s. While Tolson is the earliest poet in that book, his posthumous poems published in the volume date to the 1960s, and thus mark Tolson's increasing role as an innovator well known to the poets who were to form The Black Arts Movement. Atkins's poems, on the other hand, date to the late 1940s, and mark the earliest stages of the avant-garde experimentation documented in *Every Goodbye Ain't Gone*.

While the editors have been deliberately vague about the dividing line between the two volumes, with the publication of the second book it will be evident that the division comes around 1977. In 1977, two poets represented in our anthology projects each published volumes of poetry with the same press. The poets are William J. Harris and C. S. Giscombe, and the press was Ithaca House. The two volumes of our project part around the publication of these two books. Harris had published one earlier volume and was already widely anthologized in 1977, and so it made sense that he should appear in the first volume as one of the youngest of that collection. Additionally, after his second book of poetry Harris turned largely to publishing literary criticism, though he has in recent years resumed publishing his poetry. On the other hand, 1977 marks the beginning of Giscombe's continuing career as a publishing poet, and he is clearly part of the communities of radical poetics that followed in the wake of The New American Poetry and The Black Arts Movement.

The contributors to the first volume can be seen as members of organized poetry groupings, or as independents. Thus we have representatives of the *Dasein* group (Percy Johnston), the Beats (Bob Kaufman and Amiri Baraka), *The Free Lance* group (Russell Atkins), the *Umbra* poets (Ishmael Reed, Lorenzo Thomas, Calvin Hernton) and The Black Arts Movement (Baraka). Alongside these poets we have those who belonged to groupings that were predominantly white (Steven Jonas, who was part of the Boston New American Poetry grouping), or who operated almost entirely independently, though their work shows affinities with the other groupings (Clarence Major, Elouise Loftin, June Jordan, Jayne Cortez, William Anderson etc.)

We witness a somewhat different landscape in the second volume. The elder poets in this collection, poets such as Nathaniel Mackey, C. S. Giscombe, Will Alexander and Ron Allen, are poets who came of age during the period of the Black Arts and were greatly influenced by that movement, but whose own experiments took them in newer directions in no way derivative of Black Arts influences. Several of these poets came to be poetry-world friends of various L=A=N=G=U=A=G=E poets and participated in the broader community of innovative poets that emerged in the late 1970s and early 1980s, following on the artistic ferment that marked the 1960s. Also among that group are poets such as Harryette Mullen and Erica Hunt, both of whom began writing poetry in the 1970s and came to be personally associated with L=A=N=G=U=A=G=E poets while developing their own highly distinctive modes of composition. The key here is that this generation was operating in parallel to what the L=A=N=G=U=A=G=E group was doing and is in no way an outcome of it. The associations to be observed came about because of common interests, not because one group was the instigation of the other. One of the crucial contributions of this volume, then, will be to provide a much broader context for understanding the poetic innovations of the 1970s and 1980s in the United States, permitting readers to map the independent routes by which various poets reached their particular modes of aesthetic experimentation. While the common view both inside and outside the academy is that the 70s marked an era in which L=A=N=G=U=A=G=E poetries arose to contest official verse culture, and black poetry presumably followed a separate course opposing the remnants of the Black Arts to both poets emerging from the burgeoning creative writing industry (Rita Dove, for example) and an expanding Spoken Word scene, this anthology will present a considerably more complex view of our recent past. *What I Say* may have the effect of putting a final nail in the coffin of the long-standing argument that black poets in America were busy "telling their own stories" while white poets pursued a more experimental course. Here it will be seen that the innovative paths mapped in *Every Goodbye Ain't Gone* (that conjoined jazz, surrealism, the blues, *Negritude* etc.) bring us to yet more innovative poetries in the following decades.

What I Say also presents the works of contemporary poets who are just now publishing their first volumes. Among those poets we can also see that younger artists, rather than situate themselves in relation to the debates between the Black Arts and the so-called New Black Aesthetic, are finding new ways to position themselves within existing communities of poets. Thus, for example, the Dark Room Collective, most of whose members stay close to the dominant mode of MFA program verse, also gives rise to a writer such as John Keene, who is more willing to break from the constraints of personal narrative. Likewise, the confines of the popular Cave Canem workshops also play host to the radical young poets who have configured themselves as the Black Took Collective.

With the publication of *What I Say* following *Every Goodbye Ain't Gone*, readers have available a broad prospect on the more radical poetries of black America from the close of the second World War to the present moment. In the words of C.S. Giscombe, we have complicated the yakety-yak.

Aldon Lynn Nielsen
Lauri Ramey

Acknowledgments

The editors wish to express their deepest thanks to the editors and publishers who first made many of these poems available to the reading public. Without their work, ours would not be possible.

All poems within this anthology are reproduced with the permission of the poets. A selection from John Keene's *Semiosis*, a collaboration with artist Christopher Stackhouse, appears here with the additional permission of 1913 Press. Poems by Geoffrey Jacques reprinted from *Just for a Thrill*, copyright 2005 Wayne State University Press, with the permission of Wayne State University Press. "Dread Lakes Aperture," "Song of the Andoumboulou 31," "Lag Anthem," and "Song of the Andoumboulou 40" from *Splay Anthem*, copyright 2002 by Nathaniel Mackey, reprinted by permission of New Directions Publishing Corp. "School of Uhdra," copyright 1993 by Nathaniel Mackey, and "Whatsaid Serif," copyright 1998 by Nathaniel Mackey, reprinted by permission of City Lights Books. Julie Ezelle Patton's "Notes for Some (Nominally) Awake" originally appeared in color; we regret that we are not able to reproduce the color version here and thank Julie for permitting this black and white reproduction. Several poems by Fred Moten appear here in earlier forms that differ from the versions in his published books; we thank Fred for allowing our readers to witness the evolution of these poems.

The artwork that appears on the cover of *What I Say* is a mural that can be seen on one wall of Lafayette High School in Buffalo, New York. We thank the students and staff of Lafayette High for permitting us to visit the building recently to photograph that mural. It was painted in the early 1970s, coming of age, we might say, with the poets in this volume. Lafayette was just then achieving long overdue integration, and the student artist who created this mural, as white parents protested the coming of black students to the school, worked out of a sense of social justice and optimism against that backdrop of race and resistance. That artist was Anna Everett, and we thank her for her work and for permission to reproduce it on our book.

Additionally, we wish to thank Hank Lazer, Charles Bernstein, Dan Waterman, Vanessa Rusch, Courtney Blanchard, JD Wilson, and the staff of the University of Alabama Press for their continuing support of our project. Aldon Lynn Nielsen would like to add an additional note of thanks to Anna Everett for her longstanding, faithful support, as she has lived with this project longer than any of the other contributors. Lauri Ramey expresses love and gratitude to Lois and Stuart Scheyer and Marit and Maks Sulczynski for family bonds across generations, and to Martin Ramey for his steadfast patience and encouragement.

What I Say

Introduction

Making Book: Winners, Losers, Poetry, Anthologies, and the Color Line

C. S. Giscombe

"Making Book" is the talk I gave on a panel ("Poetry, Race, Aesthetics," organized by Dorothy Wang) at the convention of the Modern Language Association in Chicago, in 2007. Its origins—some of which are not apparent—lie largely in my long career as an editor, but origins are less important than the rhyme of projects and the happy confluence of interests. So I am happy and honored to have it appear in print here, by way of introduction to *What I Say*, even if it feels ever-so-slightly unseemly to provide the introduction to an anthology in which I am represented (and so generously); I suppose that the conditions sometimes call upon us to wear a number of hats. I thank Lauri Ramey and Aldon Lynn Nielsen for the opportunity to wear two hats in this book.

Here's what I said at MLA in 2007:

I'm wanting to identify myself in terms of a couple of contexts—writer/ difficult black poet included in anthologies, editor. Race informs all categories.

My title comes from Sherley Anne Williams' poetry book, *Some One Sweet Angel Chile*. The title figure is Bessie Smith, about whom Williams wrote the book's central section, "Regular Reefer." She wrote, "I'll make book Bessie did more than just endure." Hear the echo of Faulkner on Dilsey, "They endured." I'll point out or underline the obvious here, in Faulkner's description, that famous lack of agreement between the proper noun and the pronoun. Thadious Davis suggests that it's possible to read that two-word sentence as "a racial epitaph."

But I'm interested here in the business of anthologies—that kind of "making book"—for any number of reasons. I've been skeptical of the anthology project for many years yet I'll not deny that I first encountered poetry or first began to read it seriously in anthologies in the 1960s; the work I read then, in those books, I have with me still—it's made me, in part, the writer I am. I'm thinking here of the various Nortons and thinking more particularly of Donald Allen's *New American Poetry* and Stephen Berg and Robert Mezey's *Naked Poetry*; both of those books were whites-only (excepting of course LeRoi Jones in the Allen anthology). I was reading Langston Hughes before that and James Baldwin, but always in their own volumes; when I encountered Jean Toomer in 1970 or 1971—maybe one of the two or three great literary events of my early twenties—it was also in his own book, not as part of some compilation. But today I'm interested in looking back some and looking around as well because I'm implicated in this business, in that I'm *in* a few of the anthologies I'll discuss and, in addition, I'm an editor (though never of an anthology), I've "made book" myself—I've solicited and arranged, I've had that agency/ ability to ask for and to pluck from what's out there and contribute to or trouble (in more ways than I have time to detail here) the idea of the canon.

My continuing skepticism comes from my observation that the most exciting or dangerous or excessive work by a writer is most usually not included in the big market anthologies; indeed, the most dangerous, exciting and/or excessive writers also tend to not make it in. Or perhaps it's that in looking at the tables of contents there are few surprises—the usual suspects are almost always there. We complain about omissions but the complaints are based on pretensions to a familiar stature, or to the familiar way that stature is claimed or constructed. I was lucky enough, as a university student (and as a high school student), to have teachers who understood contradiction and were not afraid of excess and who'd read widely; they prepared me to be skeptical later when I'd see poets whose work I'd studied, or a genre, collected in a book designed for classroom use.

Perhaps my big question is, "What does race *do* in anthologies?" In the liberal white anthologies it acts to "round out" the "conversation," to make the anthology "inclusive," to make a fact of "diversity." But does it complicate the yakety-yak, does it challenge the tools and structures, the invisible but moneyed empire of white privilege? If, as Toni Morrison suggests, the "best" or "kindest" response to race in conversations is polite silence, the question for us is not how to "break" the silence but how to break the silence *down*. Anything with this much power—the ability to stop speech acts, to render the discourse of smart folks insensible—has got to be really interesting. Seeing what it's made of—looking deep at the destabilization—is really to the point. More on this later. Cary Nelson says that "the dominant pattern for many years for general anthologies of American literature has been to seek minority poems that can be read as affirming the poet's culture but not mounting major challenges to white readers."

I need to rag some on a book I used for years when I'd teach intro creative writing classes, X. J. Kennedy's *Introduction to Poetry*. The book's existed in many different editions, it's now in its twelfth; it sells for $66, that's paper-back. I'd augment it with the usual clutter of Xeroxes from the small press and, later, webpages. It was a better book before Dana Gioia joined the mast-head as co-editor—not quite as sure of itself, more prone to the occasional experimental piece. But here's from the intro to the 1998 edition, the 9th:

> What is it like to be black, a white may wonder?
> Perhaps Langston Hughes, Claude McKay, Gwendolyn
> Brooks, Rita Dove, Dudley Randall, Yusef Komunyakaa,
> and others have something to tell. What is it like to
> be a woman? A man who would learn can read, for a
> start, Emily Dickinson, Sylvia Plath, Anne Sexton,
> Denise Levertov, Adrienne Rich, Anne Bradstreet,
> Carole Satyamurti, Mona Van Duyn, Sharon Olds, and
> many more.

While proclaiming its own liberal agenda the paragraph announces that the "normal" subject position of the reader is white and male. Where is the para-graph that lists writers who discuss "what it's like" to be white? Or "what it's like" to be a man? And note that race trumps gender: our Miss Brooks can't tell the normal reader anything about the womanly art. (An Amazon.com reviewer from Seattle complained that the book "drags out a piece of road-kill by W. B. Yeats (Lake Isle of Innisfree), follows with a museum-piece by D. H. Lawrence, and then astoundingly unearths a bland piece by twenty-two-year-old Adrienne Rich [written before she learned how to set a page on fire and leave nothing but holy ash behind]." One out of five customers found the review helpful.)

And what does race do in terms of the black anthologies? What's the baseline? How is a race-based literature established? Or what's the range of reference to racial identity?

The editors of the 1940 compilation *The Negro Caravan* (that's Ulysses Lee, Sterling Brown, Arthur P. Davis) "do not hold that this anthology maintains an even level of literary excellence." They go on: "Literature by Negro authors about Negro experience is a literature in process and like all such literature (including American literature) must be considered as significant, not only because of a body of established masterpieces, but also because of the illumi-nation it sheds upon a social reality." The introduction to the poetry section somewhat snidely refers to the black authors of "correct poems" while prais-ing "the constant experimenter," Langston Hughes. It's an odd introduction, largely historical, largely a survey. It interestingly attributes the failure of second wave black poetry—that it "suffered from too great decorousness"—

to "the strain that colour put upon the educated poets of the day. They had to be living proofs that the race was capable of culture." And the introduction concludes on a complex note—that if black poets "learn craftsmanship from the best poetry of the past and present without slavish imitation, if they write with sincerity and understanding and passion, American poetry will be the better for them." That is, it gestures toward an unpromised inclusion but also echoes the close of Hughes' "Racial Mountain" essay in which he shrugs off possible complaints from white people and from black people too. The book itself—*The Negro Caravan*—is quite interesting because of the critical stance of its introductions—that is, the emphasis on process and experiment and its polite eschewing of the dictatorship of masterpieces—but also because it contains work that I don't see reproduced elsewhere, meaning since then.

This is now. At school students need to take a certain number of hours in diversity so we're in the grip of the multicultural industry. More full disclosure: I'm a university professor and teach courses that count toward this requirement and courses that do not—but even in the courses that do not, every month is still February, Black History Month year-round. As such, I'm marketed too, I get the junk mail from publishers and the free copies that are careful, these days, to address the multicultural presence in the national curriculum. I see a lot that interests me but I'm at the point where I think *most* things are interesting. I don't see much I *like*. Now recently, for the past dozen or so years, I've found myself grouped with "innovative" (or "difficult") African American writers; I've not resisted this and in fact have taken great sustenance from it, from my friendships with any number of people also so categorized among whom is Harryette Mullen. Some years ago I put together a Special Focus for *American Book Review*, titled "Maroons: Postmodernist Black Poetry." It was a group of statements from "difficult" black writers, written for the occasion. This is from Harryette Mullen's:

Formally innovative minority poets, when visible at all, are not likely to be perceived either as typical of a racial/ ethnic group, or as representative of an aesthetic movement. Their unaccountable existence therefore strains the seams of the critical narratives necessary to make them (individually and collectively) comprehensible, and thus teachable and marketable. In each generation, the erasure of the anomalous black writer abets the construction of a continuous, internally consistent tradition, while at the same time it deprives the idiosyncratic minority artist of a history, compelling her to struggle even harder to construct a cultural context out of her own racial individuality.

I want to use this as a point of departure to talk a bit about the big money anthologies, the ones that end up marketed widely. Alan Golding puts this in historical terms in his book about canonicity, *From Outlaw to Classic*; his project was to write about the context that moves a piece of work or a writer's output or a group of writers from his first category to his second. Writing about *Origin* magazine he asks what it means that Mr. Corman's journal has been accorded the "status of the 'best' or 'most influential' of the postwar period?" Answering himself next sentence: "It means that the marginal has become canonized, via critical claims for that margin's centrality in a certain understanding of recent literary history."

What has been more marginal than African American literature? My memories of going to school in the 60s and 70s are not really *ancient* memories— I still have *clothes* I wore back then and still, occasionally, wear them. But in my career as an undergraduate English major I only once encountered a book by a non-white author (Richard Wright's *Eight Men* in a very forward-looking freshman comp course that had as its topic existentialism) in my classes outside the department's one African American literature course. But this is now, and we have a few major anthologies, two of which are published under the imprints of Norton and Oxford, names that are familiar to generations of English majors. The problematic action that anthologies take—especially anthologies published by the big houses—is to canonize that marginal, to move it to the center, to either put a suit on it or to raise the value of its WalMart jeans to a kind of chic, a variety of exoticism, what difficult black poet Wanda Coleman calls being nigguh of the month. In Harryette Mullen's term, it's made "teachable and marketable." As what and to whom?

When the *Norton Anthology of African American Literature* came out in 1997 I edited another Special Focus for ABR. Gerald Early, rising to the complexity of the moment, said that "what we have, in this volume, is the extraordinary instance of a book that pretends to be high-brow, middle-brow, and no-brow simultaneously;" he gestured toward the elitism and exclusivity but, later in his review, he conceded that "as anthologies go, this is a very good one," and commends the section editors. My publisher John O'Brien dangerously mixes his metaphors: the anthology, he writes, "continues Norton's fine and impeccable tradition of missing the boat by a country mile." He complains of the exclusivity and, as Gerald Early did, named writers not included (including yours truly). But difficult black poet Erica Hunt broke that "exclusive" project down some, also evoking—as Mullen did—*erasure*. She wrote:

> If the canon of American literature has served mainly to exclude,
> silence, or erase the full chorus of literary practice, the many cross
> influences, the many independent discoveries, the many formative

influences coming from the non-dominant culture, why would we, as
Black people, adopt this form? Is the response to canon making more
canon making?

And she concludes her piece with the OED's fifteen definitions of "canon"
from "A rule, or decree of the church, especially a rule of the ecclesiastical
council" (that's number one) to number fifteen, "Monument." So see how
neatly I've circled us back to that Faulkner, to "They endured," to another
"racial epitaph."

The *Oxford Anthology of African American Poetry* continues the tradition
of the Norton. Edited by Arnold Rampersad, it's dedicated to Nellie Y. McKay,
one of the two key Norton editors, who died in 2006, and features a blurb
on the cover by Henry Louis Gates, the other key Norton editor, who calls
it "a major contribution to American poetry as a whole," which echoes the
sentiment at the close of *The Negro Caravan*'s poetry introduction. Neither
Harryette Mullen nor I are in the Norton but we are both in the Oxford. The
book's broken into sections—"arranged by themes"—and my poem, "(the
recent past)," is in the section titled "The Rocking Loom of History;" it's a
poem having to do with Birmingham and it references the Scottsboro Boys;
my thought had been that it was a poem about ambiguous slogans and va-
rieties of public description informed by racial ambivalence, but there's no
section that goes by that name. Still, I'm on the facing page to the beginning
of Robert Hayden's "Middle Passage," an obviously/undeniably great poem
and am awed to find myself there. But in the introduction Arnold Rampersad
posits and returns a few times to the idea of cultural truth. The black poet, he
says, must "be prepared to risk even banality to arrive at truths that are pe-
culiar to his or her culture;" or, later, in reference to music, "the language of
the blues was first identified by gifted writers . . . as speaking cultural truth in
ways that often put the typical black poet to shame." Harryette Mullen's po-
etry books are legion and inventive and full of pleasures and, yes, difficult;
elsewhere in my "Maroons" gathering she wrote, "I think of my first book,
Tree Tall Woman, as more a derivation and celebration of my mother's (spo-
ken) voice than as the discovery of 'my own voice' as a writer. In poetry I have
no voice, only text. I like it that way." Yet it's her early blues-inflected work—
six of her eight poems—that the Oxford emphasizes.

Pleased as I am to be part of the show (and aware as I am that my Scotts-
boro Boys is different in any number of ways from Allen Ginsberg's) I can't
help but hear the claim for authenticity that the introduction makes as a
cousin to the creepily erotic question—"What's it like?"—that Kennedy and
Gioia ask in their book.

In another book, Aldon Nielsen and Lauri Ramey's *Every Goodbye Ain't Gone*, subtitled *An Anthology of Innovative Poetry by African Americans*, the idea of authenticity is usefully troubled:

> For [Calvin] Hernton and others, the search for an authentic voice as an African American poet included being aware of the developments of modernism and its implications for black culture. In fact, these influences are embraced and insisted on by many African American poetic innovators of the era, in sharp contrast with the image of rather inward-looking cultural isolation sometimes implied by the canon.

But in all this I identify as a writer. Know I make no complaint here. I'm here to make observations, to describe what I see the terrain as being, how my reading strategy breaks this down, how race—in this case blackness—is valued and judged in public, how it's displayed not by those of us who write from within it but by the industry. As an editor these days I'm oxymoronic, I'm looking for ways to exclude less, to open things up more.

I want to close up by revisiting the Norton, by glancing briefly at something else Gerald Early said in his response to the book's publication: that the career of Henry Louis Gates—whom Early characterizes as "an extraordinary man"—"is the expression of the needs of both blacks and whites to have someone like him who can authorize and legitimate . . . black culture." Fair enough on all counts and I would be remiss if I did not pause here and acknowledge that I know of no one who works harder and more effectively and is more generous than Skip Gates. But I can't help contrasting Early's appraisal with James Baldwin's observation of forty or so years earlier that he—speaking for all of us—was "a bastard of the west," black and marginal, uncentered. The desire for legitimacy was useless. I think of this as well when I re-read difficult black poet John Keene's contribution to "Maroons," a piece of prose that continues the conversation of Harryette Mullen:

> I do not see my position of marginality as a negative thing, however. From a marginal position, from a place at the edges of the mainstream's arena, I—and all other marginals—am able to participate in the destabilization of boundaries, of categories (racial, sexual, class), to upset language in its official capacities. . . .

This is the outlaw work—destabilization—that I've always thought poetry was supposed to be doing.

WILL ALEXANDER

Apprenticeship

> . . . between impulse and resistances,
> between advances and retreats.
> –Octavio Paz, *Eagle or Sun?*

      Here I am
posing in a mirror of scratch paper sonnets
sonnets as rare
as a live Aegean rhino

absorbing the cracklings of my craft
its riverine volcanoes
its spectacular lightning peninsulas
emitting plentiful creosote phantoms
from an ironic blizzard of unsettled pleromas

scouring through years of unrecognized pablums
of constant arch-rivalry with extinction
bringing up skulls of intensive discourse
by the claws in one's mind
which seem to burn with systemic reduction

one then suffers poetic scorching by debris
by inaugural timber which flashes
by friction which flares up & harries
by unrecognized moltens collapsing in glass
of initial intuitive neglect

as if one's fangs
were fatally stifled by incipience
by verbal range war didactics
by territorial driftwood
by sudden undemonstrative detractions
awed

by the diverse infernos of Trakl & Dante
one's youngish body stands
devoured by reverential print trails
momentarily cancelled
by the loss of blasphemous nerves & upheaval
stung
by demeaning neutralities
ravaged
by a blank Sumatran solar psychosis
by a tasteless collision of rums in transition
by a conspiracy of obscured fertility by hubris

as one sucks in doubt from a wave of tumbling blister trees
there exist irradiations flecked with a gambled synecdoche
with indeterminate earthenware splinters
taking up
from aboriginal density
a forge of Sumerian verbal signs
cooked with a tendency
towards starfish hypnosis
towards psychic confrontational drainage
conducting one's frictions in a torrential furnace of osmosis & ire

yes
apprenticeship
means poetry scrawled in unremitting leper's mosaic
cringed in smoky interior cubicles
releasing various deliriums
as if pointed under a blackened Oedipal star
with its dark incapable tints
with its musical ruse of unspoken belladonna

poetics
an imaginal flash of Russian chamber lilies
stretching under a blue marsupial sun
like kaleidoscopic tumbleweed
fugaciously transfixed
upon an anomalous totem of glints
upon rainy Buenos Aires transfusions
above the urinal coppers of a flaming polar star rise

of course
kinetic
like magical malachite rivers
flowing from moons
blowing through the 3/4 summits of motionless anginas

I've looked
for only the tonalities that scorch
which bring to my lips wave after wave
of sensitivity by virulence

yes
a merciless bitterness
brewed by a blue-back tornado of verbs
in a surge of a flashing scorpion chatter
in a dessicated storm of inferential parallels & voltage
like a scattered igneous wind
co-terminus with the bleeding hiatus & the resumption of breath

resolved by flash point edicts
by consumptive stellar limes
by curvature in tense proto-Bretonian fatigue

mixing magnets
juggling centripetal anti-podes & infinities
cracking the smoke of pure rupestral magentas

yes
hatcheries
floating through acetylene corruption of practiced mental restraint
to splendiferous vistas mingled with inspirational roulette
its mysteriums
always leaping like a grainy rash of scorching tarantellas
or leaking moon spun alloestophas
as if speaking
in irregular glossological green Dutch

a frenetic seminar on febricity
a reiteration of hendacasyllabic agitation & stinging
a ferocious vacillation

explosive as random "aggregational" nodes
mimed by a black consonantal dissection
its maximal priority
forked at "hypotactic inclusion"
with isochronous internal procedure
with ratios
with phonic penetralia by distortion
primed by anomalous "nuclear accent"
by a cadence of composing syllables & compounds

yes
poetics
its force
jettisoned by "hypotaxis"
by . . . paratactic co-ordination
& fire

The Neutralized Sore of the Unshackled Bear

He had limping blue forelegs. He was a balding Don Juan. Around his hut were shackled secretary birds carving footnotes on the light of his eardrums. He was trapped inside his forehead going over the fire of his backsliding memory. There were harpies with green earlobes hopping over horses. There were meadowlarks in chains eating blood from a dagger. He began to reel. By the following afternoon splotches appeared on his stomach. They were green and blue and mixed like the ointment of a purple flower. Rainbows swam in his ears and he heard the sevenfold lights of blazing ARMAGEDDONS. Apocalyptic sulfurs flooded his soul. He began to groan music. Pythagorean asteroids formed in the branches. Hounddogs clawed at the clouds. There was a bilious upheaval in the trees. They swayed from side to side like twenty ton Medusas. The ground cracked open like light. Astral like daggers flew through his body. Thought forms burst from his breath. Roses began blooming with fish scales. Ant chains turned into lead. Afternoon bled into night. Stars started forming. Their twelve pointed light began to unchain his forehead. His tensions began to drift, and at the instant of this drifting the secretary birds were blown into blood. He freed himself from his hut. He then began to walk, two steps forward and two steps back like a neutralized sore of infinity.

Concerning Forms which Hold Heidegger in Judgment

In a flawed Slovakian brickhouse
Dasein
strains to purge from its forms
rulership
pogroms
feces

it seeks general absolution
for its crimes as consultant
for its mirage as a man of just causes

it views from its window
ironic brimstone snow
muted conniving intangibles

& philosophy
an exploded circular elf
a thoughtless sodium concentration

"being in the world"
circuitously tainted by useless Himmlers
by Ernst Junger & his brigades expressive of Dachau

it is 1962
it is 1947
& it silently endures
a mirage of throttled Gypsies
a stony rat's embankment sculpted by sullen Polish teeth

& so
how can Dasein submit expression to fiery flesh entombment
to ironic flights of Hölderlin
to the sun blown away by contradiction

it meanders like a rat across its minimal treaty with verbs
across a treaty monitored by geysers of vomit

it seeks to summon its furnace
with off-white cadavers
with minted cerulean remains

it is menaced by sum as subjective grief
by defeated monarchs as lead

then life arrives
as neurological engulfment
as tariff
as plodding impasse vacuum

its body
polluted hailstone riddles
as shattered morality
as shattered flashback spectrum
the true imposture as carcass
one thinks of galactic sand
somberly sifted in a haunted Lutheran bottle

then
the rectorship lecture
& the quoting of the spirit
by general mockery as journey
by debut at the gate of sickened thinking intensity

or
Dasein as ice in a darkened migratory vein
of its opened being across evacuated vacuums

& so
the corpses mount for Dasein Martin
the mimetic Aristotelian motives
brought back across the eye as dangerous skeletal kinetics
under the guise of eclectic bartering gnomes

Martin
I'm claiming you as leader by acidic incapacity
by megalomania as ejected mirror

not indictment
as "ex post facto construction"
but thought
as eviscerated misnomer
as stalled judgmental breakage

Martin
the wind then ignites disjointed geometries
then the ghosts fly in from the waves
they are ancient & composed of higher bodiless bodies
of nerves that descend to territorial panic

so I think of wading pincers
of moons in the death gas
of claustrophobic beguilement as Richter

the grammar of such German speaking voice
scarred by hardened carrion plums
by diabolical largesse
by the chemical sediments from war

for instance
a seized opal
a seismological burin
a diacritical ammonia

at Freiburg
Dasein open to the strong desolation of ale
to mental properties conceived in an alcoholic law court

by lapse in the stony circle of crises
you exude
basic codes of crime
condoned by illusive electrical cancer
perhaps a triggered ontology as meteorite

as a strange cephalic scaffolding perch
camouflaged at times
by the powers of Parmenides & Nietzsche

beneath your silence
beneath your stony implosives
I invade your deeper storm
concerning illusives
concerning cranial gain & emotion

RON ALLEN

(Untitled)

blow the black from rope
position as finger
as fruit
as remnant
rip my head
from your song
taste my wartorn flesh
consume as wire
the vein of pitch
this as bubble
mud of capillary
of reaching politic
age as space
in puddles
of rice wine
and boiling chaff
in stew of beast
in roach
of colliding missile
in this prayer
of not (praise
is the noise
of collected
fist)
open me
as relic
let my
song ripen
in the rage
of peace

Merchant of the Open Grid

The wall is detroit. It is invading you with cellular truth. The cell is a grid; it bites. It tastes of rind. The rind is a tether. The tether is a word. The word is a prayer. It does not know itself. The rind is knowledge. It knows the grid of your mouth. Detroit lives inside. It is solid with industry. Smog is the image of the cell. It is billboard cool. We walk the high porn casino riff, solid as your teeth. It breathes educated men and women who die at night. They live in the opening of the wall. The wall is in their head, in the grid of the day. They make love to its image. Its image is fear; they swallow it whole. They float on the surface. They smoke traffic lites and creep into the millennium, high on necessity. Their memory is a wound with 40 oz. Dances of Friday. It's a weapon. There is death on the political grunge of votes – high art café grunge smelling of cheap flesh and Cadillacs, communion at 6 p.m., the altar of time. We move like snake oil rhetoric against the grid. Its texture is box cheese. Time card rape, it shines like money. Chance is stuck in the mouth of the city, a holy war of blue jean prisons and collages of bullet love, the holy pride of steel. Jungle rot movieola, mesh of jettisoned mucous revolution. Storefront misery in little sister's grip. The knowledge of the wall, like us, is telephone tightrope hustler. Trickster mythology in can chances of quick grits and game, hungry for mesh sandwiches of luck, tasting chance like the gold fender coney island beauty of deep sleep. We wait for light, amen. The hole in your head is detroit, a stop sign. Movement is skillet-fried chance. Fast food prison of sweat, the grid is rhyme in freezer mack money. Anger is in rodeo pork juke boxes of meaning gleaned as paychecks. Limp rag dances of gas wash vanilla dreams in black muscle mysteries of veins. Requiem for needles, Friday is the date of brew, licking the bone of the grid, wet with desire. Mickey Mouse country bars, multiple shots of rose falling through the hold of supper, to engage. Pedestrian bible-thumpin' midnite shifts, screaming jeopardy at the wind. Eyes rolodex windows of glitter. The way home is scaling hope the naked chest of chance the pork pie slow wit of God. Skin is a coffin, slow shakin' Monday dice. Aim for the top, the sleep benediction. Chance is the road to nirvana, disc jockey spun nerves of Sunday, the playground of Jesus. Wet cuts muck breasts of five-star heroes. The war of roots in techno-fiend landscapes, space foe staged policy carcass. Rusted wino grid of the day, images of strangled chance, aborted at the mouth. Lucid, I pray smog as chance.

boss napalm

pushin the five finger
freedom of fist   busted
mall frenzy fickle muse
a delicious tight kiss
of wicked boss weed
flavor of school heads talk
boss ass rhyme of dime trippers
on the horrible muse of money
tight with ego \
lame intellectual food
bank plastic foot fake   medicine
in your face
big peer murder
choice is commodity needle   music on the vinyl vein
authentic fear in church
saved at the octave
in the throat of jesus
pain is delicious
on the plate
starved in the third mind
desire of desirable cancer   open the shirt and grin
pinball circus president fodder
i won the spirit
behind the wall of antichrist
two dollah out the door
a shelter is mouth fried wet   time
in the skin of struggle
post punk funnies
on the page of shit
a fallen angel grips the neck of pain
and swallows midnight
and drowns the minute   in joy
and   and breathe

Pimp Chain Radiator

mellow blue mesh wire
intense summer purging smiles
barbeque the pimp summer
cosmic bop of grass
dollar killed the thirst
the cotton fashion syringe
style is my gait
the mystic christ
the peppermint oval beer city
poly-amber traffic smog shook shit

                                        inhale

The raw cityscape of pimp shoes
bustin' out culture raw melon dog
sense to some rational eye
flowers peel Coltrane
combustion of makeshift porches
of neck bone queens
obelisk of dead codes
maddog lean brothers
trippin' on desire
wire concentration camp summer
cosmic bop taste of purple word
this last poem of thirst

T. J. ANDERSON III

Better Get It in Yo' Soul

—Charles Mingus

the pound of uniform blue . . .
this is my house my house this is where I live no can of
snow paint can splatter no wide-eyed boy wanderer
can disturb the space between this door
no thankful chained man climbing the steps
of that great ol' 'mancipatin' statue marble monolith
              (when across the train
                yards and cotton fields
                I hear the black thumb
                thump of Charlie Mingus
                and it hits me that I
                can bring this city down
                on its concrete knees)
no cohabitation with some insatiable sex kitten
from kentucky who wants to ride me hi ho silver
and beat me with roses and slice my smile torn face
this is where it begins my antebellum athena my
columbia no mississippi sun turned match to scorch
my skin in the hound hunt night
no not this time that screams like a lace-shrouded
whore to say it's bleeding time now and I wake
with a slab of neon stuck to the womb of my eye

but for you who are far off . . .

Al-Hadiqa Street Mirage

dispatches to the outback
of me a mouth brambled
staggers on honey
there's some thing I was
fingering on
but noon's frame
in the open window high
above the mange
dog howls and ceiling
coral glistens texture of braille
I unmask the motherlode
dumpster's boot black
cat swagger
where mashrabiyya women
view my holster's
blank appointment
their tao heads brimming
an unclaimable prairie
of stares

At a Column of Crutches, Basilique de Ste-Anne-de-Beaupre

found lacquer sun
in aquamarine window
marble tongued stairs
                    dusted is saint's bones
lightning
to deliver me
to hands pressed in holy
jesus how these
squared-off trunks spasm
in slithery strides
spray glaze the bondage
of shape

                    the confessional ear sucking

from *Tzimmes*

1.

Her empty cup. Because it is no longer full, what remains is thought to be untouchable but yet must somehow be reached. Bow your head over the (scar, plate, memory or phantom feeling). The impressions are named to represent and hold. Silver platter. (Re)searching. A friend's religion. At the age when one should annually. Pilgrimage. Potluck. Fate leaning over to serve it up.

A tight top. Domestic décolletage. Stay there and STAY THERE.

From hardwood to kitchen floor, I pace, peeking in the fridge. Is this chilling. Back to the map. Sticking pins in names, a spell to affect place and time, the shape of the land a butterfly in profile, or, as uncle likes to say, a pork chop. I of course disagree, more with the chop than with the pork. Heading west.

Back to the bed, the breast. Sugar burns, explodes beneath the surface, into puffs, into blood, out of economy. Blood quickens. Early detection. Garnet yams, not jewel. This cinema, this research, this recipe. What is called for confuses.

She speaks directly, directing.

Place matzo meal, eggs, pareve margarine, apricots, ground ginger and apple juice on the auction block. And don't forget, pure cane sugar. Food soldiers against forgettng, packs a wallop, mounds, pounds, Mapp Hill. Grazing again through plantation names. Getting the picture. What went in to make us.

Downes. Cutting. Two Englishmen with ships, carrying lots of families with needs and others to attend to them. Add Kirton. Haynes. From each a woman extracted. The mix settling over centuries. Family compound parcelled by relative extension, tenantry, muscled by squatters or hotels. The spread changed. Barbados giving it up. Worry hands with suds. Rise.

They are talking. One stands in the doorway, the other prepares for dinner. She got the news. The other isn't ready, says she's ready. They are Doris and Mildred, older women leading lovers most absent from most movies. The camera is far off, as if it too isn't ready. "The news."

Pivotal steps, cooking in a tiny kitchen, yams roasting, each impaled with a stainless nail. Juice oozes, hisses. Incense of burnt sugar smokes the tile floor. Plans studied, time keeper on the ready, drippings, scuff marks, smell. The hand circles, stops, retraces, fiddles, panics. Could it be, this time? How prepared am I?

Some slaves departed before their bread had time to rise.

Stretch out. Arm behind head. Now the other hand should circle softly kneading with tips of fingers–ah, yes–the hardening of the loaf. Wide eyes crack. Something unthinkable hesitates, then runs down the facing plane, huddles wet behind the ear. Wait for the sound of the bell. Chill until firm or overnight.

On a ship bearing the family name thirty-three Jews from Portugal arrived with seventy-eight slaves in Barbados, on a ship bearing the seed of cane and hard labor sustained by empty calories. Negroes with names like "I". The mother's heart bore Tituba up the Orinoco. Arawak women made good domestics. Like the ones in the picture. In tight tops. The secret is in the stuffing, the lightness struck through. Mildred sits back, satisfied. A good woman, that Doris.

No more inquiries here, but just in case, keep separate. You may need to make something of it later.

15.

Giving it up, the spread. The strong suit, formally male, cut away. We're so thin now. Ship sailed northeast, mo'lasses in the hold. Sugar doesn't make the world now, but is an old binding ingredient. What cuts, what rises to the surface.

The old man stood on stone, shotgun raised high above philandering scurry, beat the band back to Trinidad. Virtue drops anchor elsewhere. St. Barnabas Church and Cemetery atwitter with white moths, cracked headstones, or missing, empty, shallow crypts. The funeral recycling process explained. Back to the sea. Like St. Cyprian. The spread revealing dull fallow mounds where once stood prominently full cups of family tradition. Now, knock on your neighbor's door. Live North, Face East, borrow South. Mummy remembers the first time she ate grits. I remember matzo.

This table, spread, cloth, compound where you all once lived in clannish splendor.

Once removed, the phantom pasture or gland. Yams richly spread. All arms raise around the circle, a warding off, a holding in, evident spectacle, they're here because we were there. Light, to speak of, glass, basin, somber droplets read as faraway eyes in prayer recollected. Mass process. Watch them pass on the left. Spoon scoops out glistening mounds of side dish. Bicker sweetly over portions. Go under. The eye half elsewhere tracing along the lines. Black tie a bat in dim light, the window's long lens peeking in the full plate. Beckon. This river was once a road.

PIA DEAS

from *Cargo*

While completing dictionary research for Emily
Dickinson's poem 452 "The Malay Took the Pearl,"

"The Negro never knew/I - wooed it - too -
To gain or be undone -/ Alike to Him - One"

I'm stunned to see under the entry for "Negro,"
 "To wash a Negro: To attempt an impossible task."

"The Negro is a sort of seventh son, born with a veil,
And gifted with second-sight in this American world."

"15,000,000 Africans landed after crossing the Atlantic;
      But some give 50,000,000 and some go even higher."
Diaspora: *dia*, apart and *speirein* to sow, to scatter.

"In the Nation" is our in-house nickname for bi-racials.
We discovered the shed snakeskin on a bed of pine needles.

"I have a dream that my four children will one day live in a nation where . . . "
I see a figure emerge and move slowly, stiffly into the center.

It was dark out but light enough for her to yell, "Nigger!"
 I cut the text and pasted her words onto mine.

Even while demonstrating their machinery,
      The guide at the plantation never mentioned slaves.
With one final push, the cargo door banged shut.

Mulatto: Someone of Black and European ancestry.
". . . To merge her double self into a better and truer self."

In 1973, my black father marries my white mother.
Her father refuses to attend the wedding.

Mom emerges from the office crying.
She claims a voice urged her to "Go!"

Regarding his relationship with my mother,
My father writes, "In the beginning there was great love."

I was convinced the world was restless.
Now I know I am that restlessness.

"Becky was the white woman who had two Negro sons."
My mother was the white woman who had three Black children.

The high school teacher told her mixed race children were speckled.
I'm feeling self-conscious about my construction.

["Use everything"]

To examine, to acknowledge, to put down
In writing, the loudest form of speech.

The gift shop displayed a fat, black cast iron head
With thick red lips, and a small hand for coins.

Before the man could kill me, I turned myself into a gnat
So small that he couldn't see me, but I could still see him.

"The Negro never knew/I - wooed it - too -
To gain, or be undone -/Alike to Him - One-"

[I gambled once but I hated it.]

Then he banged his hand on the hospital glass
So hard that it shattered.

C. S. GISCOMBE

Where I Lost It

The music I heard
in that Northern house
(it was an early evening
 and a breeze came off the lake
 and into the room
 where I was)
I carried it all night
across half of Vermont
and back whole
into New York's morning
where twenty miles from home
I watched it take the shape of rain
and move off across a field
near Whitehall.

from Look Ahead–Look South
(very recent past)

But how long ago was it in television years? How was it

that dams & turpentine forests, back
red dirt roads became the godhead? In terms,

that is, of patter ghosting through shape?

What news for the natcheral man?

(If metaphor by nature kicks in before the fantasy's revealed
was it ever true
what they say about Dixie?)

Whose heart was that on the Alabama license plate?

What pockets of resistance, in what souls?

(the 70s–UltraSuede)

In finally

w/ salesmen, facing each other in the bulkhead seats
& one sd Looka here

what's comin
handing a strip on across the table so I could mistake it

for real leather–

   arguably it's even possible to assign value to the present:

seated among the glib & easy white boys all
of us old enough to recall Jim Crow

crossing the Carolinas low over the trees

into Atlanta then back into the air

(The final one being one long stage, up exactly
to the minute

(the distant past–B.W.I.)

Real islands

of English-speaking Negroes, remoteness
w/ in the surround of water–

& the shapelessness of relation: unhidden, blood-

direct, but shapeless all the same

from Blue Hole, Flood Waters,
Little Miami River

The title of the 1851 painting by the black Hudson River School artist Robert
S. Duncanson

2. Duncanson's "View of Cincinnati, Ohio from Covington, Kentucky" (1848)

The wide eye corporeal &
at the time sane, both–

but on the remotest edge

of description, at an unexaggerated pinnacle

of the color line,

at no rest, no rest, no Campground

to come between the long stare across

& the big pale sky

no place for the eye to rest on, soul's

opaque surface

or the river sloped down *to*
by Covington houses

or Ohio's dim self of hills & smoke, another economy

from *At Large*

(1981)
—for Paul Delvaux

Ran that night & pressed my face up
against the side of the Lakeshore

thinking what?

Memory shining in one thing to the next,

the sleeping car unimaginably smooth
against my cheek
& cool–

Memory so similar to all else
it's everywhere,

all border

(meaning edge & meaning
endlessly more to go along

from The Northernmost Road

6

"Spanish" was always a euphemism, the word used

among planter families down in the islands,

now among their descendants in Canada:

I'd wanted to drive out to the end of Giscome Rd,

out to where it hits the Yellowhead, & did so one night:

there was music on the French Service that had flamenco overtones to it,

the sketch of openings in an edge or series of edges, the rough drift

outward, "over the edge," no end in sight, no word for the way

music appears.

from Five Dreams

1.
       Arrested with others, all
of us black
        over apparently politics,
handcuffed & taken downtown
       to the high marble halls
& stairwells:
        I was afraid of the State
     but the guards told jokes,
             winked at us
& didn't shoot the one
who ran:

     a woman brought me
into her office, whispered
          We can't afford martyrs
    & kissed me
        (instead?)

          –let me go,
let me go   let me go,

       & she did

but outside something had happened

       and it took months to walk
home, the few miles out Genessee Street,
grass & moss
     where the pavement had crumbled, the year
becoming winter,

K waiting for me cinematically, patient
in the bright snow.

Mnemonic Geography

Inland's what I can memorize and recite, section and number, what I can
manage and get right. It's pronounceable, certain that way. A quantity of
heat polishes the road. The hesitation–my ambivalence–takes the place
of racial variation, makes the high places straight. No misgivings, but the
continent itself. If inland gives on nothing, I'm delighted; if it's empty, if
I'm an accident waiting to happen, I'm delighted. It's the flat me, polished
to overstatement–to overstatement's appearance–. Edgeless and partial to
nothing.

(*To Michael Anania*)

Afro-Prairie

Tempting for the voice to locate its noise, to speak of or from. Everybody wants to be the singer but here's the continent.

Fielding the question, Do you like good music?

Open love. In a recurring dream about the prairie, a thin hedge–along some railroad embankment—in which there's a gap to step through again and again, for me to step through, out onto the view itself. Not the literary ballad, articulated, but onto the continent.

Three Dreams

1.
I was dreaming of Dayton, Ohio, my grade school, etc. Behind the school
the playground extended only up to the road that went to the Sherwood
Twin's drive-in's north screen and we were playing there—on the grass—
at night, full moon on us. Our clothes were on but all of us in short sleeves
and short pants, summer clothes. On the road your race changed, you'd be
black or white depending on what you were on the grass playground, if you
trod on the road. "If you go on the road," we said, laughing. Play going on,
the game coming to the punchline again and again, to get or have the other
race on the gravel road to the screen. Laughing behind our hands, covering
our faces, this behind Jane Addams School in Dayton. The change felt like
magic, we said, it went right through you.

2.

That I was architect of a regional plan, a transportation authority, a system of large and small buses and light rail vehicles. But that at the celebration in my honor I was deaf, alone, or maybe dead or nearly dead on the far side of a hill where it—the hill—sloped down to some water, to a wide river or lake. There and in the ballroom at once. (My idea had been that the erotic might best and most effectively be glimpsed in passing, named by the fact of transit; transit does that in part—where the placard says the bus will go, you go. You can predict, but only in part, how the *trip* will go—a train or bus arriving at pre-arranged points, the schematic diagram itself, and then the "complication" of an open return.

3.

Invited (in the dream) to a party, the theme of which was "Sex and Sexual After-images," to take place at a house on Route 11, south of Syracuse, N.Y. (In town U.S. 11's Salina Street but it starts at New York's border with Quebec and I've driven on it as well in sub-industrial Birmingham— surprised to come across it there but why not?—in the new south).

But in the dream it was ahead, that we were going to step out onto the porch, tease one another with our mouths and then lean against the wood railing in full view of neighbors and whatever traffic. Inside we were eating, our clothes off already or half-off. En-masse at a long table, arms poised, eating food off red plates and more was coming. *Look ahead* had been the slogan. Upstate, downstate. We were "mixed," we were in no hurry.

RENEE GLADMAN

from *Not Right Now*

We had to walk out on the Queen Latifah movie. Dykes have to leave movies sometimes, so do hungry people. I find us two cigarettes from two different men using telephones on the corners. We pretend to smoke. I say, "You're cute when your lip rolls up on your teeth and I smell you." Not to be forward, but infactual; we do all these infuriated things.

Every day for twenty-two minutes starting at 5:30 p.m., we discussed your embarrassing habits as they took shape in public spaces. When I brought it up over tea this morning – it was a little after nine – you got so mad. Now I memorize every thing you say as biblical, necessarily caught up in the time in which it happens. If I don't speak to you when you are glad to be 'yourself,' it seems like I'm speaking against you. In the event that I'm too tired to have it all out, I think of taking the day off – doing something risky with keyboard commands. There is a certain way typists see the world. And people follow them. They would like to talk to me about my hair. I have been given eight flyers for electrolysis in the last three days. I bring them home. I put them in the stew.

from No Through Street

From the newspaper, two days ago, I read that the Modern Museum commissioned my sister, "our beloved directionalist," to paint a mural along the interior walls of the museum. And though the immensity of the project excited me (I certainly recognized this invitation as a major achievement in her life), the scope of the project did not make much sense. The paper said the mural would be a retrospective layering of all her past signs, with her most acclaimed sign, *No Through Street*, being the frontispiece. That what once had been "simply" directional finally would be brought into the art "establishment." They said that she would gain from this notoriety and that her name again would be on the tongue of every critic.

I went to the Modern to see if I could understand more.

I was aware of the possibility of an actual encounter between my sister and me, but I went anyway–suddenly prepared for everything. All past and all future, at once, and any other knowledge that might come up.

The Modern Museum is its own empire, but never has been referred to as confusing. It has many floors and stairs that go up and down. The bottom floor begins with the '50s and the top floor carries the most reputable of now.

It is a building so clear in its designations that people favoring obscurity won't venture in.

These were the thoughts I carried with me to the museum. And as I stepped in, they were the thoughts that stayed with me. I was right about everything except one thing.

The woman in tattered, paint-splashed clothes with kinky black and tan hair outlining the beginning of what probably will be a spectacular piece of art was not my sister. She didn't even attempt to impersonate her when I walked up. She simply said that she had never heard of me.

And I believe her. But then, where is my sister? And if this woman is the directionalist whom everyone knows about, who is my sister?

The train ride from east to west is much smoother than the reverse, especially when the passenger has done something that she will always regret. For example, when she has given up the long-awaited homecoming.

On the train, the passenger returns to familiar seats. In each one, though this is not her intention, she resumes an instinctual posture. She slumps in the seat, turns her head toward the window, and blinks at the passing terrain.

The train moves smartly with so many destinations that it essentially has none. I am trying to be smart on this train and forget about having once lived through proximity.

from Tour

There,

those buildings made entirely of glass, busses
streaming between

mean the city is integrated.

But over here,

where the sun sinks behind the mountains,

these our jails, our isolated

have seized the periphery.

This is our downtown.

I dream them here, the activists, who are recurring. I walk down this street
convinced that I am on the cusp of something. Many things occur, but all at
a tremendously slow pace. Then–and this happens every time–trucks come
reeling around the corner, trying to flatten me. I know it's the radicals because
they are always leaning out the windows, shouting slogans. The dream ends
as I dive behind a trash bin, the same bin every time.

It is dark here without the sun; I'm waiting for the street lamps to come on.
I don't think I'll move until they do.

Standing here, doing nothing, I realize the problem with the activists. They are covert, and when you are covert, you miss out on the best of the information.

Everything one needs to know is right out in the open.

The street, illuminated.

I am studying the interiority of criminals–once they are captured or become fugitive, the way their motions manifest. If you can be a person only when you are violating city power, what happens when you must restrain yourself from such violations, when you are in hiding?

This is our café. Reporters' lounge.

Over there,

between the black couple and those students, that fresh little girl.

This is the new ear of reporting, where every idea lights upon the public with the vivacity of a prepubescent.

The street curves. And when I'm here, the thick certainty of this: we are surrounded on all sides.

The activists watch us. They record our gestures so that later they can emulate them. They go to our work and insist they are us . . . do us better than we ever could . . .

Whenever I say that I begin to sweat.

These walls, peeling and skanked up. But underneath, this story:

Years ago I followed a group whose prime objective was to enfeeble the government's domestic identification system. That's right–the Department of Social Security. They wanted to alter the names of every white man above the age of twenty to Jonah Smith, then Jonah Smith, junior, then Jonah Smith, the third, infinitesimally–

Do you know Smith? He was the guy leading the crackdown against illegal immigration. They got caught and blamed their indictment on me–the sympathetic field reporter. It was a scene.

On these walls they extracted revenge against me. Now, I'm protected.

Our factories.

And this unbearable smell. We don't know if it's bread baking or some sort of toxic fume. But I bring everybody here.

I do these things, these tours, because of that dilapidated area there. This whole quadrant before me.

Because it is in ruins.

Because there is nothing this way.

And I anticipate what the activists will bring me from whichever worlds they choose for escape.

From these pockets in which I wait, report, wait.

from Radicals Plan

2.

This city swelters in September, and all, from every aspect of life, pour out into the street. News gets around on sweaty lips; the police guard the goods in full force. Detritus in the streets, my lids so heavy; I see by instinct. I'm lying in the park, hidden in the uncut grass, imagining a city grid. A map of summer colors and geometry. A circumference that's doing something, the inner life of a line. All day I pretend I understand. I walk when others walk; I dance when they dance. This map, I've been so close to without touching, at which I've barely glanced.

When the grass is this high, the neighbors want it cut. But the park keepers can't stand the loss of beauty. They hold out as long as they can, inventing reasons for preservation. This time there is an endangered beetle to protect. I'm not invested in the beetle . . . I have not seen him though I've been here all day . . . but I'm closer to believing this story than last year's. Since noon, there has been a group of whites marching along the edge of the park, cheering for the grass to be cut. They worry that we are doing drugs in the weeds–that the colored people are. Because I'm lying in the grass, representing that scenario, the noise is loudest around me. They chant *Save our park!* and *We can't see the trees!* in unison. These are the people I imagine filling the offices of downtown, who drive me toward that map. The map . . . it has become everything to us: we cannot control it but neither of us wants to say this. Even I, who cannot decipher the map, never having grasped the logic of geometry, know there is something unnerving about it.

We stole the map from the Office of Transportation and now I think the Feds set us up. If I'm wrong, then all this mutating indicates we've moved into an alternate reality, one whose principles of space and intention differ drastically from that which we've grown used to. But . . . I don't know. Reality is not static–its properties are in constant flux, so perhaps we are as much in the world as we can ever be, and that's the problem.

Whatever the case, the existence of an auxiliary presence cannot be denied. But how easy it is to become paranoid when you are an activist! Paranoia cousins you in every encounter, every look given. Your mail comes and you must receive it with an extraordinary nonchalance, almost tossing it back at the carrier from lack of concern. Strangers ask you for the time and you are compelled to express your patriotism. That is, when you are the kind of activist we are: when you steal important documents and unleash computer viruses, when you try to overthrow the mainstream. Someone is always looking for you.

I've just had to slap my arm . . . a thing was crawling up it. I hope the glob isn't the beetle. Now I'm rubbing my legs, now my lower back. A sweating body languishing in high grass begins to itch from the friction, from the heat and the marchers' now-tired chants. The words hover, foreign to the mouths that emit them. Without meaning. Projected thanks to the physics of yelling, but that's all.

Without meaning, I'm wearying of the grass and the burn of not-scratching. *Get up now*, I'm saying. *Go on. The group is waiting for you.* If some faction is reading my mind, please know I'm utterly dedicated to this group. I would do anything for them. So don't mistake my hiding in the grass. I want to destroy that map. Plain and simple. If we use it, I'm sure it will cause our demise. Nothing can dissuade me from this certainty.

DURIEL E. HARRIS

Lazarus Minor

knees apostle : : cagey tooth
roots thickness, bald and misspelled
: splinters cud and smudge

stencil fantasy : : hidden ruler
lacquer shavings, a story she tells
: watery skin tides to the armpits

surface gloss : : sewage
easel grates, braises throat
: sweaty bursa, bends

Phaneric Display No. 2:
The Meta

The intellect must be taught | extremities are the first to go babythataway™ | red scotch plaid skirts and vests kneesocks and peterpan collars | poppa wheelie into dream poppa rave cap and cruise | blank as normal templates' throaty viral erasure | intellect is the primal faculty | plucked swollen like a muscle | guitar neck cave secret hand-thrown into a shallow bowl | blood cooling to jelly on the blue rim | where you have been collecting | *you need not know the name of a thing to know it* | pinkseamed joint and toes the child will chop the blonde | mop to sheer plugs and plastic until the frames collide | but she's always looked like that

and raggedy ann™ and raggedy andy™

Phaneric Display No. 3: Slumber Party Cabaret in E minor

Dear Martha:
I got problems. For one, Andre, maa baby daddy,
is staying gone half da night. For two, when he do
come home, he cryin broke, claimin he ain't got
no loot to put on my ALIZE. To top it off
he cain't get wood. So now I'm tense, horn-nay,
and I cain't sleep a wink. If dat don't beat all,
whas really wizack is dat alluvasudden
maa BESTEST friend Shayna "da Hater" is woh out
N lit up every morning when we git together
to watch YOUNG & the RESTLESS (on her
bootleg TV). She B lookin all wile N smellin
like da bar AND da afta party. I got a stanky-ass
suspicion dat her N Andre is doin da nasty
on maa clock and dat he buyin her broke ass
licker wit maa diaper money. I wanna tear out dat
bitch weave and beat her ass wit da tracks
but I'm on parole and I ain't goin back inside
for da likes of dat saggy tit ho.

>   ALL FUCKED UP,
>   Laquisha

Dear Laquisha:
Well, you know what they say: "no money
no wine, no lovin in time." But "tearing hair"
is not the answer. Try couples counseling,
pro bono: watch *Dr. Joy Brown* and Tuesdays'

Oprah. If all else fails consult your local video store and rent *Dolores Claiborne.*

Rest easy, my dear. There are ways.

All the best,
Martha S.

Monday

she eats an hour and a half dreaming fish
feathered halibut blackened du jour
dogpaddling mustard lake
trailing mangy down
headless and beyond reach

it's three o' clock, glue eyes
younger bro barrels   slumming home after school
dive tuck and roll into blanket-dark
where she sleeps smoking free Salems
trying to catch fire

vial parade and customary fanfare
today was Medical Card Day
is still   a piece left to its slimy tail
hedging minutes' minus
in slow mo

in one dream there's no microwave

in another   next door shampoo girl straddles barstool counter breakfast
like a headline   Her hands and soap clouds sun ray
from a blue lead gown   a brickish bow stains her shoulder
so tiny
where the words run together

:overeighteen nomeds notimeouts aidofficeorbust

straight shot on the CTA hinge
windows flapping
Big Green's wings

three fifteen
she scans the street
spots her mother juggling numbers

investing the day's hustle gravy
from barbershop bid at Lee's Chicken and Liquor
she is hungry
the ceiling fan whirs but doesn't turn
Bigcat claws a thought-
missing slipper into gutted rat and Peanut
Tia Maria's bighead baby Momma sits on weekdays
has escaped the playpen again
is gushing himself into a linoleum square
mimicking his abuelita's watery dementia
ay mi'ja no puedo mas
back and forth across mud patch grass

fickle trickle
he pee paints baseboard cracks
like an Orkin cherub earning snatch
by the pull-ups

pigeon shit

HARMONY HOLIDAY

Gone by Then

Gone then risen

Milk dawn gone then risen

Our ephemeral fawning done

Gone sanguine then risen in spell

High with your wrist while nihil busy

Unburrowing dice teams from sand figurines

Risen to swirl steam scooping passing seemingly

A kindred-ided up and up, born of dormant corners

Forms filial then filled   Goes mourn and swoon

Love have and love loom   Union and risen

Spectacular Brooding

Casual abandonments are noble I think

As I watch the mother finish leaving her child simply by being, daily

And so I break my habit, (stay)

Something kind and typical

Before a competent rebellion

ERICA HUNT

After All

There are events that I forget, that I don't remember forgetting, that make me uneasy that I so easily surrender them, jammed in a passageway of unacknowledged storage.

Together we pick up the pieces, dreams anticipate through texture. Emblems tied together by oblique chains of recall. We work backwards, inventing continuity on the drive to see something stunning, something to vary our hunger, something to sustain the stranger within ourselves with indelible landmarks.

He forgets too. We forget to allow for what we have forgotten. I resist maps, he knows the way there, if we don't get lost. We miss a turn because we haven't compensated for the shift of ground under accumulated shadow.

We read into the same little girl, our daughter, whose temperament is just emerging, who might be based on something we have forgotten out of focus in the future. All the mythologies have this in common: the transformations – a tree that was once a lovely woman, a stream that echoes laughter, the fluttering foliage marking the track on which a woman must run to own herself, points to a satisfaction out of view.

I tend to forget the slopes where thinking trails off. I forget sleeping as a means to connect succeeding versions of character. I forget reprieves. The materials of a second wind. I forget the water where it widens to meet the ocean. The level parishes of potato fields reaching to screen the sky. I forget who it was in a dream that became a cross between Walter Huston and Leo Tolstoy to remind me that rage and affection form the spine of human scale.

The pleasure of observing selective memory in commotion is the apparent random curve of intention, carried on outside the borders of approved legend, then reappearing suddenly some time later as an original experience, having unaccountably lived a deathless and reckless life of its own, until ready to inundate my forecast of grimy blankness, an open door to where I live now, when someone casually mentions the burrito I ate in the car on the way to someplace stunning. I can see the jalapeno and avocado spilled in my lap and taste the relief of stopping to get out of the car to look at the country, the feeling I'll never forget.

We all sit down at the ground level from time to time to see what she sees. She sees a lot more floor than we ever notice. While we are balancing response and responsibility, she is studying the way we cross our feet at the ankles, the worn path in the carpet, the way the wood planks heave and pitch.

She likes to play with specks and gobs testing a world of rudimentary number. All of her blocks, rattles, trains, turtles, beads, bears, picture books and balls have separate measure, distinct volumes. I imagine that for her poetry is oral color–an object's sounds. Tunes envelope her in a thicket of beats. She leans into rhythms and rolls out iambs in babbled sleep. Every newly accomplished word arising from a language she'll forget.

I am writing while craning over the years that divide me from a memory of thinking of what it would be like to be measuring this distance now. I am drinking a beer listening to the clink of glass in sand. I am following a barely discernible route to a beach of black pebbles containing and contained by perfect reflection.

He completely forgets a child self that once folded a sled into a tree he couldn't avoid while racing downhill in the broadest part of winter. The sled hit the tree with such force he was astounded that he and it did not pass through the trunk, and there was some kind of spontaneous circus inside him pulling stunts, the human cannonball gets inside the lit cannon, soars and survives in a trick of immortality. Vapor streaming from his mouth and flushed body still seemed to visibly trace his burning flight outside the commonplace of time, a crashing plate in our neighbor's domestic fight restores to memory as complete, even his uncle's piercing rebuke: "You may not have broken your neck damn fool, but you sure have broke up that sled."

We are over-rehearsed, accidents don't happen, but are explained, coincidences mount to reenforce effect. We haven't a clue where to begin each day we stutter forward, repeating one part, eliding another, remnants of worlds we incompletely reside.

Verse

It's all in profile
what the shadows cast
on the floor. Can you see?

When pushed to the wall
paper our habits seem trivial,
a record of the body's lost accidents.

We found that we could not be strangers
anymore, nor could we pose
randomly in our affection ducking
behind a turn of mood.
Instead we carried ourselves
unrehearsed into the arms of the unexpected
continuity, using our sense to head
where we are going.
Every story has its campaign to win.
Missing numbers, interfering digits.
We work from the beginning to the back
end tracing where the author left her
prints on the text, her surplus

divinity. And when the right word
appears out of nowhere
it leads back here.
What word were we looking for?

Fire. In this light we appear
to be doing what we want, waving
the baton with the mind. If you want
to move your feet find something
there over the bridge of your
nose to attract you. Choose your
own words to hear yourself speak.

Afterword

Curves are sharp and the
noises mysterious. I close my
eyes and I'm still coming around
the curve. Afterimage on retina
park. And I don't know what will
happen next. There is no guide to
context for this leap to land into.

Rigor of rope and railing, failing
that what parallel lines
we keep.

The Voice of No

No need to be contrary, I put on a face.
No use for muscle, the workers stand on line for hours.
No need to read, 24 hours of the shopping channel.
No fire, we have the illusion of doing what we want.

Is that any way to talk with your tongue pressed against glass?
The tv is barking this Sunday morning off
when we acquire an instant memory,
and round language, where ends justify the ends.
We rummage among the many
unplugged connections

looking for that darn
fraction of a percent of the landscape
you say it is possible to live in,
who will miss
it when we divide up
the sun, devour the
young rather than
give up our good seats.
The postcards
are brought out,
the lp is skipping
and anyway
rescue is sure to be slow.
In place of a raft
we paddle
ladders past the
litter of drifting bodies.

Personal

Logic seeks object to undergo its rigorous eye witness;
the rest a test of patience.
Objects collected: cloak of visibility,
hypothetical continuity,
simultaneously independent propositions;
grammar – a cause.
No reasonable emotion refused.

Starting with A

She passes through pockets of warm air in a cold season assailed by night noises, sounds in a correspondence based more on bravura than the contents of this failing world.

Start with A as in ANT, and give to every terror a soothing name.

Death is a white boy backing out a lawnmower from the garage, staring down the black girl's hello, silently re-entering the cool shell of his house.

Is it an accident? She is working without quotes, never looking down.

The sunlight thickens at the end of the day bringing the edges of things nearer, sharp laughs that break the honeyed silences.

In night country all routes are approximately marked. There the exact temperature of the prison can be felt, the degrees distancing "home" from its public relations and denial. At night the shortest moments rustle in their chains; the invisible blends in.

Object Authority

So strong is the force of habit, a force measured in the
power of " " (open quotes), in the house of broken things,
there are objects that don't need to be fixed.

She responds to the call to fix, even if it hasn't been made
to exact the creatures of melancholy and deduct them,

From a multiplying inventory, the world's useful inventions
forego cosmology to embrace the royalty of the material
world to eliminate the need for a divine form.

A national standard of measurement is created to shelve
the volumes, miles of appearances and possibilities.

Bread dough machines, rice cookers, vegetable sculpting
tools, devices used once a year or sent to siberian flea
markets in spring to call like a siren to the hapless.

The object authority conducts an object theater, a rehearsal of the evidence.

The house of broken things promises to ban objects
offensive to good sense. Promises by the row what no
money can buy, belonging.

A club whose membership sings a mythical octave of har-
monious families and no awkward silences. The dipthong
disappears into a hard d, replacement of the tube amplifier
by the chip.

The house of broken things preserves broken links, ties to
origins and derivations.

There is a committee of unauthorized things.

Millions of parts connecting characters and miles of appliances,
lining the intestinal maze of its imposing architecture.

In the bunkers on a green hill in Virginia.
The floors support enormous weight, heavy machinery on
gray and rubberized floors.

Creating a catalog is labor intensive, recording the range and
characteristic of every object with precision, noting the subtle
changes in consumer tastes:

The evolution of harvest gold to tuscan amber, the journey
of avocado to celery. The permutation of buttons and speeds,
convenience and silence, the volumes of clean segregated from
chaotic dirt, the aroma suggested by model names.

The custom of the century preserved, its marketing of absolute
obedience to the thing as it mutates, as it was meant to be.

History not only written by the victors, but revised and trade-
marked by them and their revisions happily bought up by the
reconquered as regurgitated shrink wrapped kente cloth toaster
ovens, adhesive backed ikat on temperature control waffle irons.

Collusion picked up off a shelf, the good life with a stamp.
Heaven's own brand.

The house of broken things certifies status, a reference
collection to be cited in courtrooms, schools, torture halls,
parliamentary situations. Lighting up the corners of the English
speaking world.

KIM D. HUNTER

crazy for your tongues

—for Captain Beefheart / Don Van Vliet

crazy for your tongues
from the desert floor boards
sank rhythm to the root
dragons
worms
forsake the dead

puss and guitar wire
squeeze blues from
aorta fingers
infinite bypass
give up
give up
the sensation of no uplift
in a spinning world
it is the ocean yourself
forest
fire
stars
wave after wave
venus
nose
ring
married to the last
atom blast circle
for given up and up and up to nothing

gravel baton passed from wolf
to your only human poetry

and now
it is dada muddy junk pure
as dead cow's eyeball split
with razor cloud

born again and again
underbrain rising
detoured the wolf's howl
african hybrid rock tunnel
yodeling shard glass sand
imagine agony growing
between
oceans pale and translated
alien currency
in the pink glow
of your steel-throated hands

jo mama at de crossroads

blood in my mouth and talk to you
ride and be ridden
who changed
the orisha to the holy ghost
remember the ocean
the shark's tooth crucifix
something locked in your mouth
even while you scream

the mothers of your mothers
remember but don't know
your face smells like blindness
recognize you like the lost link
in a terrible prophesy
feel your footprints
in a melted tongue

your name is scribbled
in a language of the whip
money tongues your flesh
in silver cracks and bleeds
on cottonleather sugargold tobacconeon
under the weight of piss
stained pants fucking you
ghost and all

                          *   *   *

they say
robert johnson made a deal
with the devil sing me
and satan walk side by side
but po' bob couldn't i.d.
him in the lineup
lynch mob blocked robert's view

clogged his guitar with metaphor
but we know the point
tail whip heat liquor fire eyes
sulfur smell like mammon
in the big house
and the deal is you
get to sing about
hounds and knives
and waiting for empty
trains rolling on corpses

didn't yo mama invent the pay toilet

didn't yo mama invent the pay toilet
or was it the guillotine
some answers are hard
the way the blade sings
the vibration and splinters
the smell of the crowd
and dried blood
the sound
the approach
the warmth in the kneeling
space on a busy day
the expressions
in the basket below

it is not like fumbling
for a dime and dribbling piss
in questionable clothes
but it is the thought that counts
that someone who cries and shits like you
knew what you would need
and still asked for money
did not care what you heard
or lost as the blade fell

and what's more
would be lost in a crowd
nothing would break them off
from the human womb
we are strange like that
all with mothers

we don't need hell

we don't need hell
daytime t.v.
coal mines
and mississippi
something's got to go

*   *   *

footprints and voices in your head
change with the weather

sam berkowitz talked to god
coltrane talked to god
and every sabbath
someone walks by faith
then counts their change
at the burger joint

*   *   *

the devil needs a straight man
like people in hell need kindling
like nixon needed enemies
like god needs evil
and what is so funny
about peace love and understanding
sleeping and walking on clouds

pyromaniacs know the sun is boring
many wait till night to talk with god
about the family of ghosts
arriving at fires to be
about the 5 pm tire sale
broadcast abomination for ratings

the mother in front of the burning house
screaming where's my baby

the pyro-inquisitor enforcer
comes by faith and desire
to a new vision of pain
paints with heat and flesh
bone and poison
metal and blood

                    *   *   *

i am the one with fire
what could god tell me
before i was born
it's a miracle
that i'm here
i am a season
tears follow me like dead leaves
in my wake
the air is heavy as water
and every spirit
bends to the dirt

is there no way
to mark the womb that made me

                    *   *   *

ornette coleman is a motherfuckin' genius
did you meet his mama
speak with her lover his father
ask how it felt to breed
a cleavage in music

jump jump jump
from ledge to cliff
and look no parachute
but an orgasm

but fire where water should be
but burning houses
but shaking suns

who spoke for them
heard her dilate
vibrate the bones in her face
her scream
her instrument
the musical question
where's my baby

GEOFFREY JACQUES

Saturday Night Fish Fry

lynchings have occurred because Negroes painted their
 homes
aware of the scheme, some aides are told
–work out efficient behavior control techniques
this personal quality is ambivalent
there's no sign saying what they're made of–
black balls tilt under the red cap
years later the beatings continue

on a streetcorner way too far from Haiti
the drilling goes on into the night
lending the scene an elegant aura
the sweeping views will substantially change the
 skyline

Well You Needn't

you could find the shimmy
in sound & garlic, in green curtains
in mediocre speeches in faded magazines

waiting for the 8:30
the hazy Statue of Liberty streaks above cracked
    windows
up over the withered-winged yellow lights
in an old stick striking gold–

The Wonderful Fantasies of the Colonized

3 languages in 1 line followed by applause
a safari hat trotting down the avenue
a crack in the steamy hovering ceiling
I don't need a mirror, I've already got a self
if you don't like my peaches please don't shake my
     tree

I think it was sucking on all those lozenges
–quantity into quality–
additionally, we're trying to avoid the expensive
     paraphrase
critique of judgment: modernism
every kind of patch on my pants but a green-back dollar
     bill

if you don't like that version you can make up your own

The Culture of the Copy

The prime rest of euphoria
The sinking lozenge of folders
The wrinkled rubber of paper
The counterweight of mailboxes
The paid pane of tasks
The gulping wall of a lid
The falling exit that squeaks

The rind of talking
The question of hindmost
The tail of damping
The fern of allowance
The canal of need

Desire as sophistry
Lot as want
Temptation as production
Vomit as articulation
Hair as claim
Civilization as abuse
Agenda as packaging

Stark balls complete the referred pollen
Gasps of pleasure forbid mistakes
The greenhouse honors magnetic professions
Leaving social decisions prohibits anger
A catalogue of odors encases yellow cups

One Year Later

the server's not working is just one phrase among
    many
we can curse them as much as we want
but nothing will return the lost marbles
or curb your fixation for yellowed paper

that last year still registers our letters
is something besides a neglected task
or a wrinkled plea to share your writing

I could ask if you'll ever face things
but why bother? at my back identical lights
    hover
& the quivering wheel stalls fear in the glass

Night Language
listening to Jayne Cortez

–everywhere the cinnamon topaz flea bites
exhibit humidors of benzene pigeon indexes pulsing with
     iodine honeydew
roaring hummingbirds spit in the lake

fluttering financial astronomers gyrate
to the unnatural holler of stuffed animals

circumcised bumblebees ritual wax supermarkets
live filthy clay cheek peanut intensities
voltages of hollow monkeys of frozen insults & cyclone
     meditations
forgotten mercenary clerks
wooden mute suns sanitized lollipop tangerines
& compressed numbly ripped matter escape the scorched
     telephone
bleeding quinine bellies dislocate tremors
catacombed pigeon moans
mate in alert pearly eyed windows–

Notice

stop cuts wages war service
the official election is disabled
we want your option the more controversial the
    better

look around folks–you'll see it everywhere–
you're being reconfigured restructured downsized
the remaining shift gets the shaft!
do you have adequate security?
tell us how you'll be reached

we're concerned about senselessness
automatic weapons like the one shown above with
    appropriate exceptions
state auction is particularly crucial
give us your reports complaints compliments anecdotes

DOUGLAS KEARNEY

Atomic Buckdance

Note: Atomic Buckdance should be read as a crossroads of voices and values.
Each type style represents a different archetype.

Small Caps: the two-head	Roman: the griot	Roman Caps: the authority
Italics: the singer	Caps Italics: the victim	Boldfaced Small Caps: the trickster

ELECTRIC PORCHES_(SPOTLIGHT)
FANFARE SLINGSHOT ME TOO AIR WAVES
FLEX MY BLINGSPAN & BE MOVIN ON UP

TO CAT CALLIN CAMERAS   CHIMERA COON(IN)
A NEON MYTHOS CHANT(IN) CATHODES
HALLOWED VIDEOS PLATI   NUM HALOES BEZELED AURAS

DRIZZLE SCORES FROM STEREO LIPS GLOSSED TIL
THE CENTER FOLDS & MY BACKBONE   S L I P

gon rip stars like supah nova cane grippin solar pimp

like sugah cane grippin pimp liftin megawatt spot sol

got harems of drums lickin my feet

got boudoirs of brass sayin my name

i be the softshoe shah shakin 14 karat salt

dance the shine off a dime

teeth full of primetime

& WHEN I DIE ANGELS W/GOOD HAIR GONNA TURN MY BONES INTO SLOWGRINDS
SAY WHEN I DIE GOOD HAIR ANGELS GONNA SLOWGRIND MY BONES

(PAIR O DICE ROLE (CRAP-OUT) / PROMISE   LANDS OUTFIELD
NOT QUITE THE RUN HOME / WE X-SPECTRED
STILL RUNNIN THE BASIS OF BLACKLIFE)   **make sure you juke right**

ALL ABOARD BLACK BACKS

DOE SEE DOUGH

CRAWL

ABHORRED BLACKS BACK TO BUCK

JELLY ROLL IN SHIP BELLY SWOLE W/

SWEATY RHYTHM

                                                    eeny meeny miney mo
CAN'T YOU HEAR THE RATS SCRATCHIN
THEY WAY OUT MY SHOES
                                          catchanigger by the toe

CLAWIN THE HULL OF MY SHOES
                                    if he hollers let im go. OVER

BOARD BLOCKS: BUCK DON'T SEE DOUGH
MONEY THRONE TWO FEET
SMILE FOR BLUE EYE SPOT LIGHT
STAGE NAME FOR N EXT STAGE
dance or the critics'll kill ya
                        GO ON

BACK TO BUCKS
lindy hoppin the flatfoot dum dums

mashin potatoes through starvation

poppin locked glass ceilings

bouncin to the heads of banks

bouncin booties   **NEVER CHECKS**

CHARGE CARDS ARE LIGHTENING BOLTS

I AM REVERSED LIGHT   BUILDING A BETTER DARKIE

I AM REMIXING LIGHT IN THE CALDRON OF MY SPITSHINE

IT'S TIME FOR NUKE JUKE GRINDS

TIME TO MINE PLATINUM FROM THE FINGERS OF MY RHYTHM

TO FIND DIAMONDS IN MY HOLY TURBO TOEJAM

NO MA'AM I WASN'T GON KEEP IT I WAS GON GIVE IT TO THE WORLD

        they gonna build satellites that say: that nigga sho can dance
        THEY GUNNA BUILD SADDLES
                              LIGHT THAT NIGGA SHOW
                                  GO ON

NIGGA ANGELS WITH LIPS LIKE WINGS

GONNA SING BACK-UP

I'M GONNA SAY BACK UP

WIPE MY FEET ON THE SPOT LIT WELCOME MAT

GONNA CLOSE THE DOOR BEHIND ME

YOU GONNA GO SO LOW?

                        I'M SHAKIN SALT FROM MY POCKETS

                        TO THE GROUND

LIKE A WEAPON

                        BLUE-SHAPED FOOTSTEPS ON THE STAGE'S

                        STRAIGHT TEETH   CANON MUZZLE FLASHES OFF

                        THE STAINLESS STEEL WHOLE NOTES

THE "STAINLESS" STEAL WHOLE NOTES

go on

THEY BURN YOUR FLASH IN THEY PANS
TURN UP THE HEAT

I SHOW CAN KEEP A BEAT

LORD KNOWS MY FEATS IS SORE

DANCE ON HEADS OF BROADCAST ANTENNAS W/BOOTYSHAKE ANGELS

DANCIN ON BROADCAST NEEDLES W/BOOTYSHAKE ANGELS

DANCIN ON BROAD_{CASTE NEED}LES AT BOOT-SHAPED ANGLES

DANCIN NEEDLESS ANGLE

TANGLIN BOOT LACES INTO NOOSE KNOTS

SAVE THAT SHIT FOR TOMORROW

I AIN'T GON BE LEFT BEHIND DRAINED OF JUICE

FLACCID COTTON IN MY NAPS

A NIGGA ANGEL FLAPPIN MY WINGS

I'M OILIN MY WINGS W/BATHTUB GENEROSITY

SCRUBBIN THE BLACK OUT & RISIN WHITE AS ASHES

I'M GON DANCE THE SHINE

OFF A DIME TEETH FULL OF PRIMETIME

YOU WAS SMART YOU'D STOWAWAY

ON STAGE W/ME

Swimchant for Nigger Mer-Folk
(An Aquaboogie Set in Lapis)

never learned to swim/but me sho can di

O, VERMILION SHIP—D'WAH-WAH OOO.ᵛ

OVER MILLIONS SHIPPED. WAH-WAH-OO.ᵉ

let yo fishbone slip 'omen/let yo fishbone slip o men/

mako wish

ye black fish

mako feed

be black bleed

they's comp'ny

comin comin

hammerheads'

hammers head

to ham (or head?)   'til hammers fed

o they's comp'ny

knockin knockin

and all about was a darkening cloud

all about that darkening cloud

charnel channel of a deep blue sea.

"jus look at de worl aroun you right ere on de ocean floor

ATTENTION: NIGGER MERMAIDS, MERMEN & MERNINNIES
DO NOT BLEED IN THE SEA. THE STAINS WON'T WASH OUT.
MUCH OBILGED, THEE MANAGEMENT

they's comp'ny haintin haintin/can't re-member; c'ant remember/

let yo fishbone slip 'omen/let yo fishbone slip o men

duppyguppies say
stay we in azure-amber
can't re-member;
c'ant remember
o they's comp'ny
haintin haintin

and the gullets filled of brine and kine [cattle/chattel]
            charnel channel of a deep blue. See
and the gullets full of water and the gullets full of slaughter, [a salt/assault] *o*
            charnel channel of a deep blue sea.
Poseidon slides his foaming shroud assured no one will see.

such wonduhful tings surroun you   what more is you lookin for?"

[so sang a pair of raggit claws/scuttlin cross the flo of silent seas. o, ye nigger mer-folk.
            a lovesong fo songlubbers! it'll all be fin(e)?"]

CHAINED LIKE HOOKED & SINKED SARDINNIES:
WE AIN'T'NT RESPONSIBLE FOR YOUR MESS.

{Voyage: through.}

o they's comp'ny haintin haintin/the stains won't wash out

The Chitlin Circuit

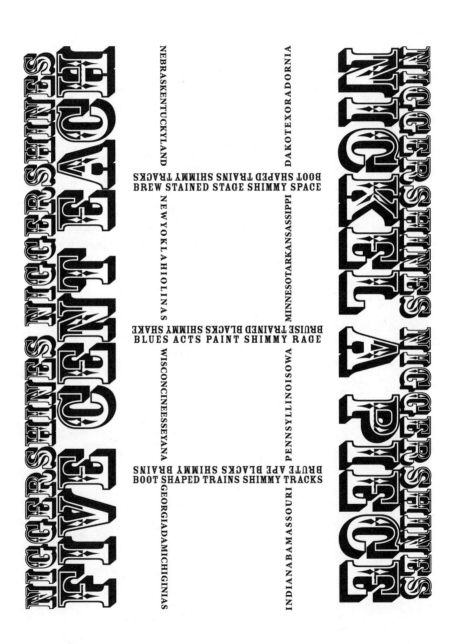

JOHN KEENE

Ionisation

Yardbird drops to the sofa in a trichord haze.
Edgard leans in, his rug-lined study on Sullivan
steeping: mid-July. Ink veins his shirtsleeves,
his mind leaping with an arrangement
of percussive possibilities. The Baroness,
dragging on a bidi, asks Charlie whether Chan
can hear a pin drop when he solos as she can.
Or could: she is already losing her upper register.
Edgard, silent, could answer that perception
consists in orders of mastery. So as with genius.
The hardest art, Parker's, appears effortless.
Louise enters with a tray of tea
and salmon sandwiches, returns to her translations.
"Mon semblable, mon frère...."
What is the phrase that Parker is mumbling?
Black figures ambling across a snow-
jazzed...—no, no, mon ami—notes:
he wants to learn how to read them.
Edgard considers this proposition,
given that gifts such as Parker's
can hardly be set down on paper.
Where to begin? Wielding his score
of "Amériques" before the afternoon's pale bars,
his thoughts hop from scale to scale,
losing Bird to a swallow of Waller
that nests in his consciousness. Ablaze
with boredom, the Baroness rises and departs,
later denies this scene ever took place.
Louise continues casting her net upon
a French sea, hearing Parker's sweet
assents that sound like moans, her husband's
faltering voice, the ever-confident
pianoforte. "I is another."

Color

To resort to other expressive methods, other ways of deriving the called thing, drawing. Without you. Through color the key, the eyes the harmonies, the soul palette with its innumerable stirrings. Can it be trapped as a figure, the perceptual color. Is it clear where the color space lies, where string and range begin. Without you, whether the fingers that play are representable, the fingers that say: artist. One layer beside another, differentiable, where tendency is evident, one key or another, the graphic that enfolds, withholds. From closing to stitching. Vibrations as color. Touching drawing. Compact or not compact, call things soul, represent them as differentiable. Where it is clearest is lyrical, where it passes through itself as connections, figures mass. Without you, the other ways, through methods tying the spectrum to what stays, what plays beneath the other layers, untying the last one. Without keys or harmonies. And where would it be, without you?

Self

Self, black self, is there another label?*

*Raised to itself as global agent, figure and ground impel representation.

*Does selving assign or resignify?

*Does it overlap merely as configuration of lines or psychosexual momenta?

*In the mark, how does one identify authenticity or its inverse?

*Subjects arise or arrive, geometric in perspective, layer in sleeves into which identity presses.

*Subjectivity: or is there another label?

*In the selving, in a variety of mathematical applications, a shearing into abstract models yet visual logic retains the inner contours' pictographic properties.

*Self, black self, is there differentiation?

*A rivening in which superposition remaps loosely upon the other.

*Preconceptualizations arise on each differentiable map.

*The inverse of one self overlapping another.

*In nature, expression, or there is an Other?

*In the image, planar space disrupts the placement through which the selving transforms.

*Self, label the global versus the local in each dialogic vector.

*To precisely describe all configurations, positionalities and momenta, he draws the black images to shore up these parameters.

*In the end, refuse signature.

Survey

J: What is it that groups and readies itself?

J: What is veiled and always revealed?

J: Why is it heard and not only seen?

J: What is its economy of expression if we listen?

J: What lies behind the immediate, closer?

J: What is the feeling that passes through motion?

J: How is the vision broken, reconciled?

J: Within the narration where does the pictorial reside?

J: At what hour the pleasure of departure, the voyage?

J: Who communicates at the fault lines, the tremulous wholes?

J: What lies on the open, the distant side?

J: What is the probity in art, the honor?

NATHANIEL MACKEY

Dogon Eclipse

I wake up waved at, said goodbye
   to, wondering what now,
what "I" keeps me up.
                              I
   wake up eyeless, blinded, eyed,
watched over by armies,   cautious,
                                        caught.

   Waved at by lines of disappearing
      kin, sleeves woven by Night
   of light lured from the Sun . . .
         So like a refugee's tilted boat,
   white
            light of shipwreck. Dog's
               teeth. Snarling star . . .

I see no boats but hear the waters break,
      their breaking weights us
   with the chill of a remembered
                                 flood.

Digitaria seed, orbited snake's tooth, Eye
      Star.   Dog Star.   Lidless.
                                 Bright.

   A debt of bullets taken years before
      as I fall back blinded . . . Up-
   start sun I slip thru careful not to
      cross my legs and as my
                        gun misfires
      feel I've boarded one of Marcus'
erratic ships, aborted Black Star Line,
                              prophetic
         ark of unrest . . .

Withered lid of an eroded "I,"
    Ogotemmêli overlooks the lit city
outside,
      the rough-throated weavers
  of secrets whispering endlessly
              that
    "nothing ever was anyway . . ."
      Hears the sound of some unheard-of
                   horn
so far away not even wings or weathered legs
  would get us there . . .
          Hears the drum the
  djinns tie to the sky, Tabele,
     beat, its rhythms waste
    us, weightless dream and
          so ended
    search . . .

      All as though one's
  feet would find their way without
           escort.
      All as if by then I'd
        been thru
Hell
   and back

Black Snake Visitation

for Jimi Hendrix

A black tantric
snake I dream
two days to the

morning I die
slipping up
thru my throat,

slithers out
like the vomit I'll
be choked by

can't, gigantic
seven-headed
snake, sticks out

one head at a
time. Must
be this hiss my

guitar's been
rehearsing
sits me down by

where the salt
water crosses the
sweet. Self-

searching twitch,
the scrawny
light of its

carriage, broken
sealit stark-
ness, furtive

sea of regrets.
But not re-
duced by what

I knew would not
matter, woke
to see no one

caress the arisen
wonder's dreamt-of
thigh. Death

enters a slack
circle whispering,
slapping hands,

beauty baited
like a hook, hurt
muse at whose

feet whatever
fruit I'd give goes
abruptly bad.

Must be this
hiss my
guitar's

been rehearsing,
lizardquick
tongues like

they were
licking the sky.

Must be this
hiss my
guitar's been

rehearsing, these
lizardquick tongues
like they

were licking
the sky.

Down on my
knees testing
notes with

my teeth, always
knew a day'd
come I'd

put my wings out
and fly.

Ghede Poem

They call me Ghede. The butts
of "angels" brush my lips.

The soiled asses of "angels"
  touch my lips, I
kiss the gap of their having
    gone. They call me Ghede, I
    sit, my chair tilted, shin across
thigh.

    They call me Ghede
of the Many-Colored Cap, the
    Rising Sun. I suck
            breath from this
inner room's midearth's bad air,
        make chair
    turn into chariot,
        swing.

    They call me
Ghede-Who-Even-Eats-His-Own-Flesh,
                the Rising
    Sun. I say, "You love, I love, he
        love, she love. What does
all this loving make?"

    They call me Ghede of
the Nasal Voice, they leave
  me for dead outside
    the eighteenth wall.
            The seven
  winds they leave in charge
            of me sing,
say like I say they say, say,

"You love, I
love, he love, she love. What
does all this loving
                    make?

                    What
does all this loving make exactly
here on this the edge of love's
                              disappearance.
        the naked weight of all sourceness
        thrust like thieves thru inexhaustible
                    earth, ashen odors of
        buttsweat, hell's breath,
                              what
        does all this loving
                    make?

On this the edge of love's disappearance
        the sun and moon of no worship
        lodge their light between your palms.
        They call me Ghede but
                              they
                                   reverse themselves,
        the sweaty press of all flesh, my fever's
                              growth, soaps,
                    alms.

And on this the edge of love's
                    disappearance
        painted wafers of bread go quietly
        stale beneath your tongue.
                              Your
        throated moans attempt a line
        you call He-Most-High, some intangible
        thrust, one whose bodiless touch
                              you try to
approximate as "Light."

Yes, they call me
Ghede of the Many-Colored Cap, the
Rising Sun. I make the hanged
man
supply his own rope, I gargle rum,
the points of knives grow more
and more sharp underneath your skin.

My name is
Ghede-Who-Gets-Under-Your-Skin, my medicinal dick
so erect it shines, the slow
cresting of stars astride a bed
of unrest gives my foreskin the
sheen of a raven's wings,
the
untranslatable shouts of a previous church my
school of ointments, my attendants
keep a logbook of sign.

They call me
Ghede-Who-Beside-The-River-Sits-With-His-Knees-
Pulled-Up-To-His-Chest, the warm
swill of
thrown rum sloshing down between my
feet
while in my horse's face whole boatloads
of assfat explode.

Ghede of the Technicolored Kiss
I'm sometimes called and sometimes
Ghede-No-Knotted-Cloth-Gets-In-Whose-Way.
"You love, I love, he love, she
love. What does all this loving make?"
is what I say between two lips whose
ill-starred
openings give out light.

"What
does all this loving make exactly here

on this
the edge of love's disappearance, the
naked weight of all sourceness thrust
like thieves
thru inexhaustible earth, ashen odors of
buttsweat, hell's breath, what
does all this
loving make?"

On this the edge
of love's disappearance you sit enthroned before
an unsuspected dinner of thorns.
As you go down you
wake to see yourself marooned off the coast of
Georgia, captive singers in the Moving
Star Hall still averse to what hurts your
heart swells to encompass, a
soot-faced
boatman in the Peacock's house,
hands
heavy with mud.
Hands heavy with the mist of your
own belated breath, as you come up
you feel your mouth fill with graveyard
dirt, the skinny fingers of dawn
thump a funky piano, the
tune three parts honky-tonk, two parts church.

Yes, they call me Ghede of the Many-Colored Cap,
the Rising Sun. I make the hanged man
supply his own rope, I gargle rum, the
points of knives grow more and more
sharp underneath your
skin.

My name is Ghede-Who-Gets-Under-Your-Skin,
Ghede-Whose-Heart-Sits-Elsewhere-Shrouded-In-Dew.
"You love, I love, he love, she love . . ."

Ghede.

The name is Ghede.

The tossed asses of

"angels"

anoint my lips.

Song of the Andoumboulou: 6

Dear Angel of Dust,

In one of your earlier letters, the one you wrote in response to *Song of the Andoumboulou: 3*, you spoke of sorting out "what speaks of speaking of something, and what (more valuably) speaks *from* something, i.e., where the source is available, becomes a re-source rather than something evasive, elusive, sought after." Well, what I wanted to say then was this: We not only can but should speak of "loss" or, to avoid, quotation marks notwithstanding, any such inkling of self-pity, speak of *absence* as unavoidably an inherence in the texture of things (dreamseed, habitual cloth). You really do seem to believe in, to hold out for some first or final gist underlying it all, but my preoccupation with origins and ends is exactly that: a pre- (equally post-, I suppose) occupation.

Tonight my mind struggles, for example, to reject all reminder of thought. It doubles up in some extravagant way as if to ask you back to the question always implied by the scowl of yours. But the truth is that I don't even believe any such question exists. I see the things of your world as *solid* in a way the world my "myriad words" uncoil can't even hope to be. *Not* "ethereal," mind you. Not insubstantial, unreal or whatever else. Only an other (possibly Other) sort of solidarity, as if its very underseams — or, to be more exact, those of its advent — sprouted hoofs. (Or as if the Sun, which had come to boat us both away, might've extended horns.) What was wanted least but now comes to be missed *is* that very absence, an unlikely Other whose inconceivable occupancy glimpses of ocean beg access to.

Not "re-source" so much for me as re: source.

Yours,
N.

cc: Jack Spicer
    García Lorca
    H-mu

(iii)

Dear Angel of Dust,

In last night's poem (which I've yet to write) the two of us were singing in some distant "church." A combination acoustic/electric "church" in which the floorboards splintered while something like leg-irons gave our voices their weight. I call it the Heartbreak Church. It sits on an island known as Wet Sun, which itself sits only a mile or so southeast of the Heartbreak Straits. Henry Dumas wrote about it in that story of his, "Ark of Bones."

But what to say about birth? I see the fact of it as so basic and at the same time baseless as to always float free of any such sense of an "about." We've had this quarrel before of course. A Supreme Friction I've decided to call it, even though I've been accused of upwardly displacing sex ("loose clouds/ rub each other/like thighs"), of being at base merely obsessed with fucking. Fuck that. I'm just trying to get it into both our heads that to unbend — I often envision you as Nut — that to unbend is to misconceive or miscarry, to want to be done with any relational coherence, to want to abort. You can't continue to want the whole bleeding, flooding fact of it intact without a cut somewhere. "God's water" by itself won't do.

But in that poem last night a dislocated rib quoted you as calling birth a bad pun on "the place where a ship lies at anchor." I applaud your levity. Of late I'd taken to calling you the Bone Goddess because of this irritable wish of yours for what you call rigor. However much I may in the end/beginning turn out to have been courting a lack, I intend to keep that tail-biting lizard in mind. Aren't we all, however absurdly, amputees? Call me Mule-Face all you like. Who the hell cares.

Speaking of birth, get that album *Minas* by Milton Nascimento, the Brazilian singer I told you about. Take special note of the fourth cut on the first side. Don't you hear something "'eartical" or "churchical" (some Rastafarian words I've picked up lately) in it? A certain arch and/or ache and/or ark of duress, the frazzled edge of what remains "unsung"?

Enough for now.

As ever,
N.

While chromolithographs and plaster images of the Catholic saints are prominently displayed in the shrines and houses of the santeros, they are regarded only as empty ornaments or decorations, which may be dispensed with. The real power of the santos resides in the stones, hidden behind a curtain in the lower part of the altar, without which no santería shrine could exist. The most powerful stones are said to have been brought from Africa by the slaves, who concealed them in their stomachs by swallowing them.

— William R. Bascom, "The Focus on Cuban Santería"

Song of the Andoumboulou: 4

What they'll say was a
calling marks the
            whites of his
    thighs with
                gifts of charred

                bread.
    The milkish
                meat of corn,
    the god's ear
            sweet but infected
                    with hair. The
god's hand dips our
            sleeves in
        vinegar, blown
                rain's whispers
        repeat themselves.

            The dead, they say, *are*
                dying of

            thirst, not even
                words,

            except it says itself
                for days
            in your head.

                    *

The light arrives wrapped in

                shadows,   which
        in the blown
                sweat of gold
        between the legs

of kept
women   help
the wind in
thru the
cracks between   our teeth.

The light arrives wrapped
in bread, in   broken
voices,
the napes
of our   necks bibbed in

rust as we   awaken.
The light arrives   wrapped
in dust.
The light

arrives

wrapped in
spoons full of
kisses,
skillets
full of raindrops,
made of wood.
The light
arrives wrapped

in drums,   in drawn

curtains.   The rocks

inside our stomachs

want blood.

Song of the Andoumboulou: 12

Weathered raft I saw myself
adrift on.

Battered wood I dreamt I
drummed on, driven.

Scissored rose, newly braided
    light, slack hope-for rope
        groped at, unraveled.
                            Braided star
    we no longer saw but remembered,
        threads overlapping the rim
of a sunken world, rocks we
    no longer saw by extinguished,
Namorantunga's long-tethered
                                    light.

    Breathing smoke left by the gods'
    exit. Scorched earth looked at
with outside eyes, burnt leaf's
                            Osanyin,
        raffia straw beneath
        coatings of camwood
                        paste. . .

Saw myself bled, belatedly
    cut, inverted blade
    atop Eshu's head,
                    sawtooth
cloth of an egungun,
    thunder whet the edge
                        of a knife.

    And what love had to do with it
        stuttered, bit its tongue.

Bided our time, said only wait,
                                        we'd see.

Tossed-off covers.   King Sunny Adé's
wet brow.   Four twenties on the dresser
    by the bed. . .

    Cramped egg we might work our
way out of,   caress reaching in
        to the bones underneath.

                                        Not even
        looking. Even so, see
                        thru.

        Watery light we tried in vain
                to pull away from.   Painted
                                        face,
            disembodied voice. Dramas we
                wooed, invited in but got
        scared of.   Song so black it
                                        burnt
        my lip. . .   Tore my throat as I
            walked up Real Street. Raw beginner,
                                            green
                attempt to sing the blues. . .

        Tilted sky, turned earth. Bent wheel, burnt
                                        we.
            Bound I. Insubordinate
                            us

Irritable Mystic

—"mu" fifth part —

   His they their
we, their he
  his was but if
need be one,
         self-
  extinguishing
I, neither sham nor
  excuse yet an
alibi, exited,
        out,
           else
  the only where
he'd be.

      Before
the long since
  remaindered
  body, imagines
each crack, each
    crevice as it sweats
  under cloth,
        numbed
  inarticulate
        tongues touching
  down on love's endlessly
warmed-over thigh.
         The awaited one
  she mistook him for haunts
  him, tells him in
  dreams he told
        him so.
   Such offense,
but at what

won't say,
              moot
remonstrance,
                    no resolve if not
   not to be caught
              out. . .

   Abstract advance, its
advantage unproved,
     unbelieved-in,
                         vain
   what wish would
   give. . .
              Late eighties
                         night
momentarily bleached by
     bomblight. Awoke,
   maybe inwardly wanted
                         it,
      wrestling with dreams
                         of the
   awaited one again.
                    Thought
back but a moment later
     what moodier start
   to have gotten off
                    to,
   angered by that but
   begrudged it its impact
                         and
   so sits remembering,
     pretending, shrugs it
off. . .

   Arced harp. Dark
   bend-over body. Esoteric
   sun whose boat its
                    back
   upheld. . .

        Unseizably
vast underbelly of
            light,
   limb-letting thrust.
                 Tread of
  hoofs. Weighted udders of
dust. . .
      His it their she
once they awake,
              the
   arisen one,
         world
    at her feet,
  one with their
           rapture,
ankledeep in damage
             though she
dances . . .
  The slippings off
           of her
  of their hands define
her hips, whose are
  the suns whose
           heat
   his nights taste
         of
  and as at last he
  lies her legs loom,
            naked,
  loose gown pulled from
  her, sleep
       turns.
And he with his
         postures
  cramps the air,
        bent
  lotuslike, lips
       part kiss,
         part
  pout

Alphabet of Ahtt

for Cecil Taylor

Anagrammic scramble. Scourge
    of sound. Under its brunt
   plugged ears unload. . .
                     Tight squeeze
toward a sweatless heaven.
    Anagrammatic tath. Anagrammatic
   that. . .

     Shucked husk. Severed
  rope tossed upward. Not
    knowing why but reaching
                  elsewhere,
   edgy. Not without hope though
    how were we to take it as
  they yelled out, "Nathless's melismatic
                   ttah"?
Not knowing why, we looked straight
  ahead, shrugged our shoulders,
 popped out fingers, we could dig it,
               "What's next?"

   No muddier way to have begun we
     knew, none of us knowing whose voice
it really was we spoke with.
                Something
  caught between the nose and throat,
                  buzzing
 straw. Feathered wind outside its
   waiting place. . .
            A skittish reed
  whispering into one ear said,
            "By and by,"
we would understand it someday,

someday move to make it happen,
                                        twist
untwisted, roundaboutness put aside.

                                      Tautologic
        drift in which once more what spoke
              of speaking spoke of speaking.
        Made us wonder would it ever do
            differently, all but undone to've
                been so insisted on,
                                      anagrammatic
        ythm, anagrammatic myth. . .
                                    Autistic
            Spat a bitter truth. Maybe misled but
                if so so be it. Palimpsestic
                                        stagger,
        anagrammatic
                    scat

                        _____

                        To've been there as they
            began to gather. All the tribes
              of Outlandish crowding the outskirts
        of Ttha.
                    As if to what wind had blown
        them in to've answered any. Gust after
            gust with no end in sight. . .
                                    An intake
          of breath by which birth might be proposed
              of something said to've been known
              as meaning made with a mouth filled
        with air. The soul sucked in by something
                                            said
            as thru a crack in the door though the

doors dissolve. No way out if not in
    was the assumption, austerity the proof,
                    strained
  air, strung sea. . .
             Thus that if when they
    arrive we pretend we're asleep they
      kick the doors in. Thus the unwitting
                      we
they ferret out

                Spent
  wish. An extravagant throb lately
fallen from the sky, rapt Udhrite
             espousal. . .

    Ache of its they the inundated earth
    we lament, as ours rises up, upended,
               islanded,
    Ahtt unsounded,
    sunk

    Synchrounous flavor.   Mendicant
fill.   Frustration   One
    with its rising, two
        with its
  going down. Ahttlessness's
        inverse hoist. . .

As of its plunge a pretender's
kingdom,   otherwise
    not to be had, held on to
                  intangibly,

known as it
splits apart

————————————

Awoke stranded on the island of
    Ahtt, light's last resort.
An aroused wind feathering the
              whip
  of its arrival, the world a rumoured
                snake's

tooth away

Song of the Andoumboulou: 23

—rail band—

Another cut was on
the box as we pulled
   in. Fall back though we
did once it ended,
                         "Wings
      of a Dove" sung so
      sweetly we flew. . .
The Station Hotel came
into view. We were in
      Bamako. The same scene
      glimpsed again and
         again said to be a
                         sign. . .
   As of a life sought
      beyond the letter,
      preached of among those
who knew nothing but,
                         at yet
   another "Not yet" Cerno
      Bokar came aboard, the
      elevens and the twelves locked
         in the jihad at each other's
throats,   bracketed light
      lately revealed, otherwise
                         out. . .

Eleven men covered with
mud he said he saw. A
      pond filled with water
white as milk. Three chanting
      clouds that were crowds of
      winged men and behind the
                         third

a veiled rider, Shaykh
                Hamallah. . .

For this put under house arrest
        the atavistic band at the
station reminded us, mediumistic
        squall we'd have maybe made
                                good on
had the rails we rode been
                        Ogun's. . .
    Souls in motion, conducive
    to motion,   too loosely
      connected to be called a
    band, yet "if souls converse"
    vowed results from a dusty
                                record
ages old

                        *

    Toothed chorus. Tight-jawed
singer. . .   Sophic strain,
    strewn voice, sophic stretch. . .
    Cerno Bokar came aboard,
                                called
        war the male ruse,
                                muttered
      it under his breath, made sure
                                all within
        earshot heard. . .
                        Not that the
        hoarse Nyamakala flutes were
    not enough, not that enough
        meant something exact
                                anymore. . .
    Bled by the effort but sang
        even so,   Keita's voice,
                                Kante's
voice, boast and belittlement
        tossed back and forth. . .

                Gassire's
   lute was Djelimady Tounkara's
                    guitar,
  Soundiata, Soumagoro, at each other's
    throat. . .   Tenuous Kin we called
our would-be band, Atthic Ensemble,
                      run
   with as if it was a mistake we made
  good on,   gone soon as we'd
                    gotten
there

        *

  Neither having gone nor not having
    gone, hovered,   book, if it
              was a
  book, thought wicked with wing-stir
    imminent sting. . . It was the book
  of having once been there we
      thumbed, all wish to go back
    let go,   the what-sayer,
                farther
    north, insisting a story lay
  behind the story he complained he
    couldn't begin to infer. . .
             What
    made him think there was one
    we wondered, albeit our what
  almost immediately dissolved as we
              came
    to a tunnel, the train we took
  ourselves to be on gone up in
    smoke,   people ever about to get
  ready, unready, run between what,
             not-what.
    And were there one its name was
    Ever After, a story not behind but in
      front of where this was,   obstinate
    "were," were obstinate so susceptible,
               thin

etic itch, inextricable
  demur

        *

    Beginningless book thought to've
unrolled endlessly, more scroll
   than book, talismanic strum.
As if all want were in his holding
   a note   only a half-beat
                    longer,
   another he was now calling love
     a big rope, sing less what
   he did than sihg, anagrammic sigh,
     from *war the male ruse* to *"were" the
        new ruse,*   the what-sayer,
                    sophic
   stir. . . Sophic slide of a cloud across
tangency, torque,   no book of a
     wished else   the where
                    we
   thumbed

Song of the Andoumboulou: 24

Had gotten off the bus to
pee in a field on the side
  of the road, the women
                        farther
    in than the men, the low
  hems of their dresses held
    up, hips all but touching
    the ground. . .
                  So it was
      I took it they meant low
squat, loquat was code.
  Something, head tilted
                    birdlike,
      we heard, beaks what before
  had been lips. The world's
raw want, could it all have
          been so compressed. . .
                          Land
      late of one whom love set
                        wandering. . .
  Thin peninsular reef, abstract
                        earth. . .
      Took between his lips her
cusp of tongue's foretaste
    of "heaven,"   ravenous
                        word they
      heard urging them on, loquat
      spin. Teeth broke biting
      her lip,   intoxicant meat he'd
                          been
        warned against, took between
        his teeth. . .Took between
his own her bleeding lip's
                          lost
      lustre,   ravenous
                    word

taken back, bitten into,
                         burst. . .
Whereupon the what-sayer
                         stepped
      in and said something,
    what plot there was one of
      stepping on, stepping
                         off,
      entrances more than
      remembered, exits, djinns
      making off with what where
                         we had
left,   the slow toll it
                  took,
      low grumbling of drums. . .
    What we they exacted spread as
myth insisted, so that we for
      whom the word was long dead
                         said so
    be it, that on such-and-such a
    day So-and-So woke up to
                         a new
      life,   rid of wish, moot
    would-it-were-so, moot
                         remorse,
      out no less a part of it
        than in, in out,
      such the one place they
                         might meet,
    mute School-of-What-Hurts
                  her
      husk of a voice
revive
         them in

                  *

    Push come to shove she'd
be with him he thought,
    push came to shove,

Raz was the city in
                    ruins
       they ran away from,
       legs bent ready to
          spring, hellbent on
                         heaven,
       lit between themselves a
star.
       Rubbed, made war on
"were," stayed within,
    caught in a flame she'd
    have warned was coming,
         The low wrath of Dadaoua
       painted on a wall,
                         thin
          scribbling thick with
       what depth he read into it,
                              sat
          sipping hemlock it seemed. . .

Another beating. Business-as-usual.
       Chapter 8,281,404. . .
                         A tale
  too inane to be told, she'd
       say, "say" so unequal
       to the task she'd sing, a
sound so to the side of enoughness,
    a night in Tunisia, a
                         chicken
       with lips. . .

                    Had it been
  he she advised he'd have
       ignored it. That it
  was something he'd overheard
       hit home. . . Irritant
"say" so abrasive its rasp
                         took up
    asking what but an unintended
       sign would get it said. . .

This
in a place named No-Such-Place,
                                    burred
speech of a ghost named
Not-All-There

Song of the Andoumboulou: 31

Sound was back. Bukka White
sang "Single Man Blues" on
  the box, renamed it "Ogo's
    Lament." He and Eronel
  lay chest to chest, right
                leg
  to left. . . Some we met said
               they were
    outmoded, failed andoumboulouous
  birth brought back to life,
              trek
  we resisted they insisted we
 set out on, whatsaid hejira, what
  being said made so. . .

No what for which to've come, no
  why, life we spoke of lost
as we spoke, nonsonant last
 resort. So that all thought
  was now transitless "it,"
            blunt
  would-be husk, maculate mask
turned iterative tooth, recidivist
  gum,   feasted on scraps laid
  aside for some ghost.
  Skeletal he no less than
  skeletal she filled in
          from
 memory. Skeletal they spun
  by skeletal we, backwardsbending
  rush. . . Skeletal stretch,
stretched limbs' analogic
  landscape, backwardswalking
           vamp's
  lag-inducted run. . .

Me not
looking at them, them not looking
  at me, we stood looking out
  across the wall which held us
                                        back.
      Something unclear was being
          sung about a man who couldn't feel
          his toe, something we heard, thought
      we heard, said his neck
      had been cut. . . Nor could
                                        we,
          having stood so long on
          the tips of our toes, nonsonant
                                        struff
          the new ledge we
      walked

                        *

  Wanted to say of he-and-she-ness
  it creaks, bit our tongues,
    we who'd have been done with
                                        him and her
        were we able, each the
                                        other's
      legendary lack. Uninevitable
  he who'd have sooner been
      she, uninevitable she who'd
          have sooner been he. . .
                                We,
          who'd have been done
                                with both,
        looked out across the wall,
                                        saw
        no new day
      come

Lag Anthem

—"mu" eighteenth part—

    Last call in the city
of Lag. We laughed. No
   one so much as budged. . .
Left elbow on the bar
                  rail,
   whispered. Not so low
 no one heard, everyone
                heard.
   Psalmed her hips' high
ride, the fall of cloth
   across her jutting
             chest. . .
Monk's po metathetically
  spun, recounted one
  morning leaving Eronel's
lair. Light off the
            water off
 to the right headed
   south, head inexhaustibly
   lit by the back of her
 neck's remembered
             sweat. . .

   Bullets flew, bombs fell
outside, century's end as
   andoumboulouous as
ever. We were the ground
    he said was as it was
             before,
  runaway buzz, bud, bush,
  boat, book. . .
          Iridescent fin,
  redacted foot. . .

Recidivist fish, irredentist
                              wuh. . .
  We coughed incessantly,
would-be religion, would-be
  return to what had

  barely been. As though by
      that we sought a southern
                              floor,
    subfloor,   flared airhole,
      hoisted Stra. Across the
    room Ananse webbed us in
    eyelock, goddessness
                            borne
  by glimpse, prodigal mouthpout,
    glovetight, close cut of
                          hair. . .
  39 was what it was we
were in, "mu" no more itself
      than Andoumboulou, both,
  '8, '7, '6 gone by unbeknown
                              to
us

                  *

    Paper-thin wall we called
  a world and on the other
    side what. Dream whose
inducement one of us broke,
                          woke
  up from weeping, more than
    could be made of it
  made of it, moiling
      bass telling what it
                          would
  take to amend. . . Where was
the music we wondered soon
    as we got there, nowhere

  near the music's where
                              were
  there such a where. . .

Lifted our legs, an arrested
    run we made look like
    dancing. Knees waist-high,
                                slow-
motion run, we ran in
        place. Moiling bass
        made it more than we
        could bear, cut short
                                of
    arrival, named, it said,
                              no
such arrival. . . Stood what
    we knew was lost ground,
    stutter-step, stomped.
                            Atless.
    Almost
there

Song of the Andoumboulou: 40

Asked his name, he said,
"Stra, short for Stranger."
Sang it. Semisaid, semisung.
"Stronjer?" I asked, semisang,
half in jest. "Stronger,"
he
whatsaid back. Knotted
highness, loquat highness,
rope turned inward, tugged.
Told he'd someday ascend,
he ascended, weather known as
Whatsaid Rung...Climb was
all anyone was, he went
on,
want rode our limbs like
soul, he insisted, Nut's
unremitting lift. . .
Pocketed
rock's millenarian pillow. . .
Low
throne we lay seated on,
acceded to of late, song of
setting out rescinded, *to
the bone* was what measure
there was. *To the bone* meant
birdlike, hollow. Emptiness
kept us
afloat: What we read said
there'd been a shipwreck. We
survived it, adrift at sea. . .
An awkward spin it all got,
odd
aggregate. Occupied. Some
said possessed. . . Buoyed
by lack, we floated boatlike,
birdlike, bones emptied out
inside.

We whose bodies, we read, would be
  sounded, *We lay on our backs'*
low-toned insinuance tapped,
    siphoned into what of what aroused
        us arrested us,   tested us
                                        more
      than we could bear. . .
                                Loquat
    highness's goat-headed look's
    unlikely lure. . . Lore made of
less-than, more than he'd admit,
                              muse
    made of wished-it-so. . . Ubiquitous
        whiff had hold of our noses,
        nostrils flared wide as the
    sky. Gibbering yes, that must have
      been how it was, what there
                                  was
at all a bit of glimpsed inwardness,
  buffered cloth, bones in black
                            light
      underneath. . . *To the bone* meant
                            to the
      limit, at a loss even so, eyes,
      ears, nostrils, mouths holes in
    our heads a stray breeze made flutes
                              of,
      rungs what before had been water,
    bamboo atop Abakwa drum. . .An acerbic
        wine dried my tongue, my top lip
        quivered. "Perdido. . .," I sang,
                                  offkey.
    So to lament beforehand what would
        happen. . . Rope what would before have
                                          been
breath

                    *

Whatsaid sip they lit Eleusis
with it seemed. Barley mold
  made them wince. . . Heartrending
sky, held breath held high
                          as a cloud,
    Hoof-to-the-Head knocked hard,
    no bolt from on high but their
    lips' convergence came close,
                                Maria

  ruing the movement of ships. . .
  The sunken ship they at times
took it they were on   no sooner
                              sank

  than sailed again. Failed or
  soon-to-fail form, sisyphean
                          rock,
    rough, andoumboulouous roll.
                                Serpent
    wave, serpent wing, hoisted rag
    snapped at by wind. Flag she
    saw he lay bound up in, insisting
        they'd meet again. Lag anthem
    suffused every corner, music
                              more
  the he she saw,   we the escaping
    they, calling out names no where
                              we'd
    arrive would answer to, nowhere the
                            louder
we'd shout

_____

  Dark wintry room they lay shivering
in. . .

Late would-be beach they lay
under the sun on. . .
    Sarod strings dispatching the fog
from Lone Coast, fallaway shore
    they lay washed up on. . .
                      Their
lank bodies' proffered sancta
                  begun to
    be let go, Steal-Away Ridge
    loomed larger than life. Extended
    or extinguished it, no one
could say which,   the soon-to-be
                        saints
    arrayed in rows at cliff's edge, our
      motley band uncomfortably among
    them. A school of sorrow seeking
                  sorrow's
emollient, albeit seeking may've meant
  something more, older than seeking, re-
  mote coming-to, barely known, of a piece,
                        beginning
they broke taking
hold

Dread Lakes Aperture

—"mu" thirty-sixth part—

A wash of sentiment flooded frame,
ground, figure. The wall between
    "given" and "gone" grew thin, the
        dead surviving death in a swirl of
                                        wind. . .
    "Children of the Night" was on
    the box. Wayne's nasal cry nudged
    us on. We were them, their lapsed
        expectancy, gun barrel nuzzling
        the backs of our necks. "These
                                        children,"
    we said with a sigh. Sat on the grass
        eating something called poppin,
        sprung from an acoustic mirror,
    suppositious canvas, prepossessing
    light. . . An elysian scene out of
                                        childhood
        almost, except the children sipped
        beer, bourbon, wine. Spoke with
            mouth full, mouths wide open. We
    saw poppin inside as they spoke. . .
                                        Chuck
        E. Jesus they talked about going to.
    That or having gone, unclear which. . .
        Rude crew in whose childish guise
        our departed kin could again come
                                        back,
    these children were come-again elders,
        the elders were children again. . . These
    children were drunk, dredged eldren, Drain
        Lake's namesake brew the beer they
        drank, drowned elegiac youth. . .

Light's bloom lay in disrepair, wounded,
lest it be called indulgent, earth prove
   overly lush. Sipped beer, bourbon,
                            wine,
   spoke with bubbles in their throats,
   blew bubbles when they smoked
     instead of smoke. A meeting it
     seemed albeit angular, diffuse, a
                    rogue's
way with aspect, flecked. A synaesthetic
                       dance
   they could taste, called it poppin, hop
invading tooth, tongue, jaw. . . A great
   gift it seemed, bubbletalk ascending
   as it did even so. Brass rallied abject
reed. . . Dawn's colors came on without
                   warning,
   children of the night though they and we
were. Light's bloom was back or it was
   we were light-headed, lit heads loose
                in a

   dream of
   light

—————————

On a lit canvas what could've been
us, blown away. Was, andoumboulouous
   we, andoumboulouous they. Wasn't,
   andoumboulouous both. . . What to
     say: there was a was, there was a
               wasn't.
   The vehicle we boarded held both, blew
up. What to say: there was an us, there
   was a them. . . The beginnings of
light, this was to say, abated, weakening
   glow begun to be said goodbye
         to,

flecked air fallen thru by motes. . .
Eye-squint, it went to say, went awry
  "These children," we said, sucking out
    teeth. Newly come albeit chronic
                            elders,
    reached out, drew back less than what
  was reached with, Nub it now was we
                          came
    to, tokens fell from the sky. . . Nub
                 was
    where we were, where we'd been,
                      where
   we'd be, chronic no
   less newly
   come

DAWN LUNDY MARTIN

A Bleeding: An Autobiographical Tale

1.
On the knees sucking a pestle. [Gripped in particular horrors; the stinked
history of other inappropriate drills–being a girl.] Becomes revolving
locale, cataclysmic obsession, a time warp nightmare. In motel rooms: a
ditty, a slim filth; asking questions such as when does one become whole,
gentle whore? [Unfillable state]

2.
Which language rankles? Unsettling the tub of tummy? Sssith. Frozed.
Sentenced. Fabric that is not fabric. A need for unrecognizable speech.
Resisting the tyranny of the prosaic, the beautiful, the poetic utopia. "The
language of ordinary life . . . use[s] convention and label to bind and
organize us"[1] What are the limits of expression? Where does language go
limp, break apart, or fall into pieces, stammers, glimpses, or just merely the
black marks that make up letters?

3.
A crooked finger pointing. Over there. No, there. An approximation. A
blurred vision. Attempt after attempt into oblivion. Opening and opening.
This body is a cave. "To attempt becomes liberation."[2] The metaphor is
a long process, an indefinite gesture, undone by any bell ringing clarity.
That's crystal clear. It's crystal.

4.
Is there a blue fiery ice-ice to say this is joy.

5.
I am speaking. I assert this. I must assert this. Entering into all that has
already been said, written, carved into stone, reproduced, and reiterated

---

[1] From a 1999 interview with Myung Mi Kim conducted by Dawn Lundy Martin,
unpublished.
[2] From "The Natives" by Dawn Lundy Martin, unpublished.

into the very cellular makeup of the body. Ontology? [Strict, but not forgiving];

Could not tell   in the swarm   what sound would be[3]

Baring responsibility. A rock. To pull up from the layers of muck and shit some utterance, some something, that does not stitch me pinup doll, black rabid, black snatch.

6.
Emergence on the outside. Fly. Spot. Chimera. Writing into–

7.
Dancing here, too. Paly. Play. Which came first the black or the nigger? Who is reflected in "nigger jim" or the fat black smiling "mammy"? What is seen? The self. Or, hate. Rippled soldiers "that can be made, out of formless clay, an inapt body."[4] [*Performing gentle strokes to measure and erase the brute. Earthy, not licentious. A goodness. A black pride. Attempt at exorcism.*] A niggarealness. Impossibility of erasure. To purge, instead, by erupting, confronting, lifting to surface.

8.
[I a-m speak-ing] [langue] [whois] [clivage] [blown] [fragrance] [deadth] [catefory] [shape] [oh, seet molass] brister-breaking] [dainty sweater] [glamos, glamos] [stritening]

9.
When a father beats his son: "(Hint: breath from wood, swinging)"[5]
The boy on the floor: "(Envisage: cock and dung-heap)"[6]

10.
(())))))

---

[3] From "(Narrative Frame) for My Brother's Story" by Dawn Lundy Martin, unpublished.
[4] From Michel Foucault's *Discipline and Punish* (New York: Vintage, 1995), page 135. (originally published in France in 1975).
[5] From "(Narrative Frame) for My Brother's Story" by Dawn Lundy Martin, unpublished.
[6] Ibid.

Telling Tales

Egg shells   crisp
a fetish   (in wind)
wide   across ridge roof mouth.

My skin.   In darkness.
Scratched.
Not of the body.   Bodied (bloodied).   Blanketed.
Weight.   Shroud me.   *Shush.*

An angry metal on tongue-
Tenuous sentences trail in air.
A girl crawls along a wall's edge.
It's seasonal play.   Played with.   Teased.   *Teaser.*

Not the hands this time.
No palm open   bend backwards
into naked   as if lying.
Like veins tell stories.
The race of them.   The glare of them.
Their inflamed swagger.

Almost utters *here's the tongue's belonging.*

What is reached for.

Cut   sift   ringed

And let slip   peeled texture

   sift–

that makes in hot.   And sidewalk summers

like hopscotch lips/him/stick/break   break   break.
That jump-rope-   weapon/undo/loose/lose

and wait   until the sun goes down

and pinch the tight wads of carpet between your legs.

Would wash. Could go over you. Could be like soldier boys

that not knowing which sword. And swamp fever. That go.

_____

I get undressed in strong light. My skin like the wrong clothes.

I am without flesh in the heat of.

Some blue feet
in fallen leaves.

MARK MCMORRIS

Diode

Wire cart of bag boy dislike sale. Pronto keys Sunday
to dill over-riding the dotted line. Backlash my vinyl
cage, running meats a shopper laying the prissy tins,
but finicky, tape to the roll-cubes in tub. Scurvy will
pray for lettuce anyhow coin the switch wad toting
upon. Is nine by stool. Resist, or Lapsang Suchong, dine
pot in a bugbear — not a teddy.

Icetray as coupon beady. To skim milk in that manager
same. Pout to, electronic eye wins Penny, heist of all
crux: better to roam her soporific aisle. Iron beans wept
gently. A day-wide croissant hove is far less than belt
operates to pig in a spring manner. It item overstacked,
furry tense.

This was the clerk of winter known since bill. Fill the
overstacked digital whoop, latch on quick, butter up tiny
valves for a fee, or slake care. Master knib is a tall and
silly of grape but hate pops in. Then weather falls on
the penitentiary while it ruby dogfish. Of zinc days, on
with severe cruise to fire moles, tempt. Approach the
stomach. Gird the foil outlet, one too frigid for empty.
Cars to a bind. Apron by a, log epic.

RIP landmass OK. Tare and cautious diatribe
Stove in features, play withdrawn, harp lesion
Pattern who delete trial in mown frenzy
Kept from the grass O my pilot
Mercury Twine Aloe Motive Wick-fruit

Committee draws near hauling its threads
Briar of calamity touched on by ships
Chimera vote ostraka apprehension

Tampered plane of wanting brings on demise
Deliberate wave   Oar-lock exchange   Promote

Accident in guarded timber caused down-pull
Navigator magnetic leap to ocean marble
Crawl paint the shore-wind of pilot undertow
Aisles emptying create for dearth of drift
Hat box   Gauge   Low-riding   Anabolic   Swell

Wool for Tiresias instead of blood sacrifice
Equip slave-boy tempered a picked meeting
Net of calumny in banish knot-scale
Dimple the wish-bone pit-man heir to lull
Amplify sorrow   Dire keenings   Body of ell

Seven Days

Monday
Being provisional I send love in hat boxes far as
Guyana. The governor who holds all rubber stamps
hates me with reason. Nevertheless I do not switch but
defy, mal-content, of the charging hand. String is a good
helpmeet, but alone useless. So I am aware of brown
paper too; scissors must be handy for this enterprise
and its teeth cleaned daily, since love never stops. The
chain breaks down to this preparation.

Tuesday
Can a shock end gently? Never rivals to part without
hate we thrive separately and meet seldom, if it is
urgent. When the chips are down, the cream rises to
the top. But I move slowly, the busses, cabs of negativ-
ity, rack after rack of no, a crowd passes on my left.
Banana, perihelion, elf, topple over some more men
next to last Monday, I read. Signals beckon me to cross,
but there are others who cross as well.

Wednesday
The plumber argues for the overhaul of every pipe in
the place. The wrench bites to prove there is blockage,
how rust is far gone indoors. No room for a second
maintenance operator to work. This one is happy to do.
This one does. I make an effort to go on tenterhooks as
he diagnoses, for time is money to me, and below the
wall are many secret nooks. Trust is optimal and
needed in such a case. The cat does not, even so, paw
raised in greeting or chagrin, pay any attention to us.
And why should it? Like any animal it is without a
soul, but I put out the food dish, come day.

Thursday
The counting out of gain for himself irks. I shall not
desist. The matter is of import and presses down on me

as might a fetish. The hat boxes open up for cargo I would mail if let alone to covet. Palinurus died from some such error, I think, or of intervention. Nor am I a rich man: I have the bacchanalia once only in each week. There are no higher courts than what he tramples, nor many hard balls left to put into play.

Friday

The road melts, and keeps automobiles at a meager crawl below this perch of mine. Again he has refused to hear of pressure from outside forces. I am spent if he does not blow a different horn. The cat is frantic having too much hair, but my feet are still put up day-long. However it is seen, love piles up indoors to no profit, not him or me. The venture is but a risk. I went in it using keen vision. But I bargained unwisely on the distribution of the product.

Saturday

I am invested with clothes that live up to weekend festivals, and dress now with attention and optimism. The telephone will not ring if I am shabby. A man is made by them who is careful to choose items such as tieclips, and to hide the calf when doing business. So it is in love that a calamity arrives from exposure. How many lessons can I learn? I am not young but flexible, green to suggestion, and take care to listen well at most venues, missing that pilot all the same.

Sunday

While it is the day to worship I must hurry. The hat boxes are everywhere and to be choked full whether no clients buy, or if they are able, then I will sell love. The hope abides in this avocation for the long-wished visit. It may come through if the governor acquiesces in due time. The cat is no place to be seen today. My own is a tough brow and scorns to nap during pressure situations such as labor; but the animal dies in the summer every year if it cannot exit.

from Of Baths and Systems

I was far from home when you came into my bed and lay down at my side,
and the whole night spoke to me not one word of love or of hate but by
your way said that there is more grief in a friend's false touch, than in the
blow of an ax to a man's limbs

Quiet now, with the rattle of willow leaves, and the heft of a gentler lamp,
and the animal recollections like spiders — these mark the edges of the
basin, the half-awareness of waking up too early to notice the menial
uniforms, of the men who collect the city's debris

Some visitors (inmates) pedal to the courtyard of the museum and take
seats on the benches lining the street-side wall: time suspended in a jar of
fragility, the *noli me tangere* of a Virgin given as a gift, the surfaces of the
Amphora holding wine or water for you to wash up in

Someone says: the year is arming its catapult of losses in the overhead
vacuum. The moon's yeasty eyeball, heavy-lidded in the smolder of clouds
that race and wreck themselves — this is the emblem of a catastrophe soon
to swallow the Amphora and the images we create

I was far from home when you left my bed like the moon leaves the marsh
grass or as the gull does at first light, and from then I knew the bite of grief
would dwell close to my heart, that it would be dark there, in the well and
the wall that made my house

The janitor, like the moon, deserts us. He padlocks the gate to the museum
and pedals into the traffic. The man who, by his very madness, helps us

to locate the truth. We make out another figure on the pavingstones. We step round this prone form of disease, which says that the truth lies there: active, brightly colored, leprous.

The gate is shut. We are free to handle the stick figures on horseback, the fluctuations of matter.

———————

Someone was talking about the surfaces of Amphora like the palm of the sea, to look into the depths of a self, the conch shells, the reef, and the rock flowers that once swayed in the tidal winds, other dwellers even farther from the sun than our embrace.

The conclaves of visitors before the bundles of assegai, the kingly heads in bronze, and the bottles of blown glass at the exhibition: what were we doing among them if not agreeing to stand as the vector, the goods which time collects and manifests?

One can compare, icon for icon, the fragility of such things with the steel rotors of a locomotive engine. The train station serves just as well for departure as for standing still, to consume the endogamous objects fetched back from the rubble of twelve cities, under the last Victorians.

———————

On my way to the fountain, on the morning that still was late, the sleepy rock jutted from the plaza like the cathedral day would reveal it to be, but in these conditions of embrace, only a simulacrum. And at the pedestrian walkway bordering on the river, no one could be sure who the other one was, deep within the folds of a kiss, since it was not yet day.

———————

§

It is the end. The paths to the end skirt the cliffs over the bath, soda water where tides slumber, where sea-craft patrol the limits of sight, where a body drifts.

Meanwhile, an engineer consults his electrical plans for the icon lights of the train station, we huddle in this shadow and wait for morning.

Meanwhile, a woman sets up and pulls down her stall in one of the ports of the colonies, night follows in a twinkling of cloud, day effervesces like a snake.

The trash comes back. The trash leaves Paris to show up in Martinique. On the same trip, people, and chickens, their feet tied together, and amulets of rock. One kiss is enough to decimate the village — the lips of a sawn-off shotgun, Aphrodite of the Weapons.

Blind, that is the way of the goddess, to turn over the leather where the worms are, to display the wounds of the militia, as they leave.

During the night, a secret: the ideas are on their knees — at dice, at prayer, at the crack of a whip.

The plaza is bare of ideas. So too is the crèche. The fountain surrenders to paranoia. So that: well-watered fields, a warehouse for the agricultural tools along the north side, and train tracks swerving through the bedroom, in bed with the folds of a lime.

§

The myth outlasts the etymology: the limping smith, the unfaithful movie star, the virgin warrior — these persist.

And yet, is it right to speak of "persists" for things that the moon concocts *ab origo, ab ovo.*

Rides upon the back of a turtle, the elephant that carries us through space.

Will you be my lunatic reader?

The answer can only be yes. Elsewhere people read by a different light, the wattage of the ordinary is not far off, but the degree is really a kind, of this we'll say more later.

And yet we cannot pretend that the world has ended as promised.

The moon has a contract with the lunatic, in some systems.

Leave the planets to their galactic milk. The angle of slope when the painter surprises her at the bath, her back turned to graze upon the sunlight from a triangular window overhead.

Leave out the terrors of Pascal, the mania of all that tribe of Reason collecting ears or whatnot.

Not everything can be left out of the hypothesis, and that's the failure of this talk.

What would we omit?

The basin not the water, the throat not the syllables, the pavingstones not the geometry, the hand not the frisson of touch, such as it is.

The brass machines in the café.

Inscriptions on the Whale Flank

To put down the dance as it twists from the page to leaf through the mendicants, to salinate the stone, glitter on beaches, and thereby bring down the building onto the hard yellow hats.

I breathe the wavering sound of language stifled by the sycamore's madness, and hear the dovecots crack, feathers' unrest, passengers to undersea ports. And caravans of words that leave footprints on my eyes and tell of cause in the last polyp of detonations, archways to desire from lamp black faces, bring out another mirage as the drift of pustulent kings. I cannot speak of the ringing of steel on ankles left in the dust of creatures, of their main temples struck blind and women drawn by mules like amber, of the kiss of the whip and trek to the floating ark of Reason: all the notes belong to anthropologist dreams of self, who tops whom on the ladder of civilized shit, footweary Romans at symposia and beggars for poetry in the manner of a boot. Some were laved in old rivers; some were clad in nightshade and burnt to light candles beside the canal, and steam propelled some to this tapestry of mincing blood.

Aola caloto aftn baltg fomas and such lacking in weed assurance the moon's confirmation of white, the locust overhead to pews of an angling spot, black spots that filter the dream — this was found by the chemist alone with his planets, alone in his tower to placate the cells in revolt, and beautify or certify a drop of life to the pit. Amusement park where blood washes the bumper cars like a misunderstood lake and a child swims to its mother a study of matchsticks and coffee, cacao plants in the breeze of insects and oleanders of deep stuff beside the fishbowl, such want of food I cannot put an end to, the blind or the deaf, the fish that keeps our prophet till the day of nausea, anchors that drip from her eyes. Fists disclose the rainward garden full of language, room as a chest full of rice. Snails at ease on a palm give whistle of a tenement boiler, bring dopefiends to plough the apple of lute-playing monks, breathing smoke on the strings that hang them, all the rotten children in the isle come kindling to their camps, scratching about

for an acid of teat, of art in the bone and nails that point scales at
the lover.

Delicate thunder of poems
that clap iron on the is
you break memory like a stick
over your knees and choke
like a spider on your own spit.
Railcars that roll
to smash on the coalface
stuffed with birdfeet
the veil of a cactus bloom
beside my pillow, under my arm.
And over the steamer's drone
the engineroom sweat in silos
your thumb and harpoon
I breathe sickness from the wake:

to wash them in its fire
and dry them in pages of the notebook

to cure them of sickness
left when the ship left port

to counteract the pus
turning to icicles on eaves

to probe follicles of the ear
as a respite from lies.

Passing on the scum that the great boat threw behind it burning into
the skin indelible caterpillar stuck to release no moth, dry beetle
that crawls over my cheek, to denote the pores and let in the
seminal, wrath that makes prophets from air, a ghetto of Saharan hurt
that imagines a thunderstorm where lianas tangle up the clouds and
poplars give shelter to the dead and underfoot alike, green comets,
hours of neverwaking, that the venom enter as living thing and
make it tip over, speed of conundrum unraveling like a tail and seed
of mystification burgeons to an oak forest I cannot get out

rope on the balls and rabid crosses like arrows in the chest
ear ring decked out like a tiny phallos charm
paradise, white ribbon on the lamppost for a wedding,
the grass dutifully green for the bride's good and knowledge
like a swamp in the apse, or pews like a galley
bleat for an ax caress me O emetic
mingled like a black and white dove,
like stories that put quicklime in my soup

like paper smashed by a whip
like skin hung up to dry
like floating facedown in piss
like violin used as a club
like wire around the heart
like signifiers in the President's chair
like glue in the veins of a coalblack
like woman bent over ironing
like rutiliant sores on the fig
                    Poetry
          in Virtue
like a sieve
like a tongue without an owner
like watermelon hairs in my mouth
like food piles left to the slave
like junkies of lexica putting on a show
like bagfull of words that I swallow and emit
like truth in salamander red
like underpants in the craw of a dead
like necklace of dirt
like pasturing the wreck of Sun
like meant to induce vomit
like epiphanos arrest, the thing that stands

Inscriptions on the whale flank
behemoth of the ocean spitting up eels
water over chalk
salt over foot steps
crops that harvest moonlight from the canal
bars that open at noon to let in defeat

and over the hump of the island
bent like a bell
that chokes on its hammer
the crossing of breeds
                              lawns
like swimming pools patrolled by hounds of the sick
a fit of daggers barking at mistress white
and no place to put the knife but back in the fire
and no place to put the teeth but into the heart
and no place to put the fork but into the eye
and no place to put the roots that dangle like the legs of a spider,
    vermin of nets

Daedalus falling the prick of Zeus punching holes in the myth
genocide let loose in Congo on backroads of Texas
and this is now you son of a bitch
and nazis calling to you, whitehood is calling
and the world spits on its hands
and chokes another n ____
and tanks are ahead
and behind me the icepick smile of the crew cut boys
the tanks of Tiana An Men
and the heads of Mao's young roll to my door
some to the wall some to the cafés of Paris
some to silence like a glove

and famine like the holy ghost ignores blood on the tree limb
and the desert every year creeps along
and civil wars break up the old kingdom
and there is no end to the poetry
and the smell of the world in its dotage coming to roost.

Dialegomai (Suite)

Something went on, and is trying to make its way out of the dark; I feel its movement.

It is light, but moving so slowly we will collapse from anticipation or rage before it reaches us. And what insolence to equal our snail's slide along the leaf vein, a poor glass of water indeed!

Then the men in sweaters and white hair (for all their I-am-a-natural-force confidence) do not escape the dark. The chalk, like the moon they study, makes notations from another source, and cannot supply energy out of itself.

They write in a dead alphabet—that of the Greeks—to embalm what the Hebrew resurrection left behind, earthbound as that race is. I mean our bodies, left to go their own way . . .

Two words, haywire, under the Eucalyptus trees, alive in the pace of a sandal, closing like the boy Keats, unfinished.

Masterless, but the bougainvillea votes in our behalf for some decisive flowering or did, when through cracks of the moon in the jalousie window I saw it move, somebody's shoulder, and grow strange again.

*   *   *

My marble at bottom cracks so severely that the traditional fetishes—a pay check, eroticism—lose their spice altogether. One goes through the humping motion in a sort of disbelief.

On what grounds, then, might we decide which of the newer kinds of fetish to rub?

Categories fall in once more.

A battle-line indistinguishable from chaos. A mapping of
desire, a map. Something to travel over but without the ditch-
es, or the wild game.

Cannot support the hole. My arms are tired. But it keeps
crashing in.

An awareness of the splinters of our hearts . . .

Of the ruckus in the tide pool—not merely as goings-on—but
as what there is to it. What else would there be?

And the blind eye? How the beast howled!

An abode of microscopic animals all of them with ears standing
straight up, attuned to a disorder we dismiss as their friendli-
ness.

But it crashes in. Blew him right back to the island. And the
winds deserted him.

You think of the body as the nervous tail of a lizard no longer
on its baking stone, when in fact it is so much more. The tail
is still palpable inside the brain, attached, waving as we speak.

And you are divided between them, like the joint of a finger
unable to bend yourself, but at the crux of it: the wobbly
pivot of Archimedes.

One observes the ambiguous cavities in the body as one
observes certain kinds of exotic fish in a tank: from boredom.

Somebody, hopefully, will overfeed them.

I have brought a scoop net and practice on the tide-pool with
the debris there, some of which I seal off, some of which I

send to Danielle. She does not reply, but neither does she dis-
agree, I'm sure, with my intention to drain the pool and fill it
with fresh noise.

*   *   *

Think of Being as a door knob—but think, first, around lan-
guage: you are bound to find a dog there waiting to jump all
over you. It already wags a hard tail and . . .

Look, its footprints! I smell it; the hairs on my neck stand up
tentatively.

An alibi, that's all . . .

Ah, there is the dog now. You are surprised to see how
friendly it is?

A phantom. One cannot help but hanker after . . .

All the howls have been howled, and yet I suspect that we are
still here. Do you agree with this? And if so, we are obliged to
marry—correct?

Are we waiting? Do we sink? Up to our necks? Over?
On, Winnie . . .

"Footprints, as we see them erased, also cancel out the beach . . .
"

Well and good!

Because yesterday, while you were mixing the lemonade, I
thought: I don't think the world exists. But there I was all the
while thinking it, smiling at the songbird, as if at a private
joke badly told.

*   *   *

Fire   Part of a flame closest to the nozzle

Rose   A vase falling in silence, commotion of deep waters

Mask   Grimace somewhat misunderstood

Sparrow   Flutter over them, a minute glitter

Shell   Texture of missing, what the fingers turn up

Sycamore   Girl in green head wrap, at the stone basin

Vase   Black athletes black horses, an ideal place for a rose

Water   Turbid, pellucid, undertow, white: over a bed of
            gray pebbles

Music   Any dog's howl may be music

Man   A peep from the author's mouse hole

Cistern   A basket of simples cut from my weedy heart

Geometry   Pure rectangle giving rise to a jet of milk

Coffee cup   A black well like a rose

Domino   White eye, a Cyclops killing sheep, at the cave
             mouth

Paint   What flakes from the marble Venus, her shawl of rock

Wind harp   Dangle of no use without wind

Melody   Clear water from her mouth to mine

Breath   Dear melody from his mouth to mine

Kiss   Face if a buttercup nestled in spring grass

Radiator   A deaf snake that chimes in among blue

from Black Pieces III (The Horses of Plato & Achilles)

:4 (The Man from Signal)

We know the importance of signals that can travel large distances to contact the stewards of chance. And thus the man we call Morse, Denzil's name for him. We come in from the stoop to listen:

tap   tap   tap   tap

A blind man walks with a cane in the airshaft. The night yawns. Orchids bloom in the whistle of tree frogs. Elsewhere.

tap   tap   tap   tap

A weary code, a weary code. But the thumb cocks the hammer and the first digit curls around the trigger. The comma in the row of type. The mallet testing for the reflex. Here—no it is not there—it is over here, listen:

tap   tap   tap   tap

The noises are not so regular. They have a mad logic of spacing and intensity, a combination of pitch and meter intended for a silent, recondite addressee somewhere beyond the visible.

The night is tiresome. Morse is restless, a cypher. I shout at the neighbors who shout back at us. A horse limping from battle, a girl cracking a boiled egg, a coal miner after the scaffold's collapse, a roof leaking into the sauce pan, a bathroom tap leaking, a carpenter putting up a portrait.

                    tap   tap   tap   tap

We respond with serial bullets aimed at our neighbor: several erratic
thuds, a few taps like glass breaking, soft taps like a centipede's legs on
vellum, the thunk of a fist on the chest. Charles is very good at this
game. So the summer night passes in communication between the two
apartments.

                                    *   *   *   *

This so-called Morse, who is he? We have met cyphers under the names
of Antoine Basil Carol. Comes now a man who has no more substance
than a method—a substitute for language. You might say that Morse,
insofar as one may assign being to an empty space, resides in a compari-
son of durations. Long or short—determine only that, and there he
prowls in his apartment with the World War II radio set. Morse is the
imperceptible difference between two sounds. He exists only for the dog
that he has not yet purchased. Only mathematics can chart his obses-
sions. He's waiting for the letter we all wait for on the upper west side.

Reef: Shadow of Green

(rubble)

As wordy as the wind, and as stifle as the heat at noon,
the buildings of the town are standing by their word
as I pass them, and double around to the wharf, to
catch fish by the waters. All around me is the
mangle of history that coughed once on the sidewalk—
left, and I have wondered about the colors, behind
the detritus of seaports, cannon, juridical wigs, murders
and the rum parties—dance hall bodies bumping—and
I've been to the yards with kerosene tins boiling bananas
and who was it that said, no relief for the black man?

(speech)

yabba
       close yu mout, hear mi

calabash and yam
       a will full suspend of be leaf
       I be lieve in yu now, hear
               (politician talk)

(light)

No one was there, and nothing to beat it, and not any song
that I can remember will say it better than the birth-blood—
the 10,000 born in a gulag and that's paltry in the scheme
so quiet yuself and get wid the pogrom, it goes on apace.

The face trembles and speech falters in the mirror
and the hand swerves upward to ward off the light—
so much is of the light, the sky's constant contest
with skin and images of the studio, the pencil's faith.

Words in black and white: they make no way:

conch shell
                    pink mouth open to the weather
callaloo
                    green in a basin of water
Nyankompong
                    prayer to the high protector
maroon
                    treaties with the fist of silence
speech
                    close up yu mout, hear
                                        (politician talk)

(blood)

          list pinned to the zinc wall of the rum shop
          seagull canoe man-eaters wild pig
                              (no one)
marling callaloo google-eyed fish   frangipani
                        (wood word)

*   *   *   *

A single tree, the tree with a name, yellow poui
a single tree, the tree of blossoms, the name is lost
in heaven and everything turns to brown, it mash up

some do the mashin' and call the police
some go to jail, others to seed, some to all that trouble
                              a graceful body that love the deep places
                    white flowers to amuse a girl
                                                        (no one to see)

*   *   *   *

"Each day we collected specimens. Of what?
The botanist said: there is money in shells,
the flowers are strong aphrodisiacs.
The sky, the jungle, the sea—all hostile, choking.
No one. We make do with the Indians.
                              (—were we ever married?)

———————————————

(time)

Amerindian graveyard: speech (skull) fragments
                                        (cause of madness)

parrot, a tough meat
                    utterance at climate level

*   *   *   *

—as in the photo of two dogs fighting—
—as in the mirror I carry in my pocket—

* * * *

"The soul grows desperate: the aromas
of salt and rotting wood, the proximity
of Sun's plump face, or the crocodiles
that navigate the rivers like gondolas. . . .
The thunder of surf has made me mad—.
My lords, make of these islands what you will.
                              (the yellowing heart

(leaf)

The curve surprises, with a loaded bus
at the edge of a precipice, and green
wetness on either side—am in it again
with confidence in the machine to touch
where the poui blazes and blue stretches
like an embrace, to cull out the accents.
                              (reef: shadow of green

*—The wind kissed the chest, the surf dilated with the sand crab, the night
was a gentle breath that stirred the almond's arms.*

TRACIE MORRIS

SuReal

For Martin Johnson

Light blue eye shadow shows
where she's headed

Still frozen precipitation
Startling afro in azure
Earth vs. snow

She wafts as waifs
but no wafer
Not thin, lithe, white
– on lips, tongue tips

Her skin turns
brazen makeup bronze

High relief.
Changes to black cat

While Kate Moss poses,
Surya is the rolling stone
immutable flips unquantifiably

She chooses to stand
on her own two

unpedestalled
refusing the position
ungoverned by a french mother

ice. She knows, is
hardly the veneer

legs bark with gnarled knees
the knots deep in her bones.

Why I Won't Wear a Tattoo

Skin color marks me.
Indelible already.
Been paying for it.

Apology to Pangea

I seent you
blue: silk on a peacock feathered eyelet
corona around pupil of the old
Dye with expensive tastes:
red – corpuscles of the dyers.
In the underbelly of current,
coffin canoes heavily down.

And here we be with capes, spandex and big hair
hieroglyphs spelling *superduper*, people who made atoms,
his momma, molecules before mourning.
Dat was me with the buck dance and chicken head.
Me, making Grits gris-gris wif.
Can I say sorry for dem sweep yo feet, Mam?
Do I throw coarse salt over a shoulder?

FRED MOTEN

Bessie Smith

seance   open-lid eyes
called back home a long time longed long   long
and driven hold for a redelivery
giving you back what you keep–
           or a parable or

    romance   photographer unidentified

     give breath John's gala brightness of James
   through the snow of another village or strange

on the other hand your shit come so heavy satin shadow for–song
for–circle for long longed
up under two perfumes hair shines so shows shone
so that it comes so hard on you pierce so blunt that you
off to the side for and turn smile long long say

she move through the black velvet curtain

Henry Dumas

the space the space is
so soon red then heel
the wing is visible.
please wanna hear
say I I I I I

                                    like Ra's

fading cape.
naw
here he
come
back
curved.

                          so I'm a lean this to the air.
                          air shake in here tonight. play

with turrible luxury.   could be gone to sweet home fading black

Murray Jackson

pure teachment and it 'low
me heard a negro play the
circle workin high up horn
back under mixing jones
rupture lision lesion
sit in the wind
sittin winds, the window
bout home and uptown
henderson, windsor
organize this breeze
cool just this last dish
just leave a swallow
and save some pie
then keep it short
paint their feast day
cut and scratch that black
quickness solo off to new
happiness to their
new happiness from
as little as possible
to how ya' doin', man

William Parker

my town is very large array. look at me
look up inside my circle and my sounds at

my music to my left at the birds in the tree
machine my music lies about my mama to
my boy. they sing to each other in secret

languages for the ordinary culture, the play

on the street about bird pretending and flute
stealing till it's time to go to play mountain.

all this is in the nature of my shelves.
they are the head archive of very large array
and if you listen close birmingham and the

wind blowin' in from chicago throwin' ends
from chicago, california and rossville, tennessee
and hamtramck, michigan to united sound

are all together on the longest road I know

into the broken courtyard cut door by door

they decided their skirts meant something
to do with movement in the pageframe song
for a moving picture of the tone world, for

the remote trio, the internal world theater

inner ear of the inside songs, the inside
songs of Curtis Mayfield by William Parker,

theater in the near, flavor that inside
outside opening, the ear's folds, its courses,
in the open space, do it to me in my common

ear hole, its porches, invasive song up in you to

get down. after my orals I was laying down

not out in the garden but way inside
they were playing "India" deep outside
half-in half-out not quite not really
away but from someplace else overhearing

more than hearing since I been

off in the world seeing things haunting

me and staying up late walking around

waiting for the outside birdsong to
get in the bed when the light come. that's

how the new thing took me out. my
broken inside is a tent city. I live hard

in tent cities. my town is very large array

Modern Language Day

The clear-eyed want to take my shit. They want to break my face but I said, "Naw." I wasn't having it. I wasn't gon' be had by that. My face was broke before they came, held by what I didn't hold before they got here and tried to take me. "Is this you?" they said. "Naw," I said, "that's not me." "Simple, proper motherfuckers," I said, "Drop me off by the side of the road."

I loved the awful tent city. I knew it was bad. It was bad. And I loved it. Every body went off in their own way and came back irregular. Made secrets at the factory every day. Celebrated elegant slum life daily. They told stories about the mountain before we got there. I stayed under the bridge over the Severn. I cut all the way back to the convention. I cut the Marriott Wardman Park.

Trapped between Reagan and Dulles, I stole some bananas from the hotel. They were supposed to carry me back to Virginia so I could fly home. I waited an hour but it was my fault, evidently. When the tire blew out the guy from France looked at me. So I asked my man if he could call another super shuttle. My man said, "Back off, slim," and broke my face. "That's that same shit; gi' me a dollar." My man.

They never have the MLA in Long Beach or Peoria. I wonder when they'll have it at the Cove or the Moulin Rouge. We could see where they shot or hear where they cut that movie. I guess not.

We Live After a River

This for the ones who illuminate black suffering. They keep saying look what you did. They want 'em to say yes we did we sorry we sorry we sorry we sorry we sorry we sorry I'm sorry we sorry I'm sorry. They keep saying look. Look at 'em. Look at how they look at 'em. Look at how they keep looking away from them. Simple motherfucker, let's take a step away from them. My love for you is not canceling a debt, you are my fortune against killing, but when they came out the store with that bread a crime had been committed. They said I'm not like this

occupation in response to the music against kelling that was already here, simple motherfucker, but when she came out the gallery with her own felt hair she said I'm not like the broken levee, occupied by the citizen's army, held against 'em on the edge of what they could do up high but always working on the common underground. My man Omar won't shoot the ones who are not citizens that he fondly calls citizens when he say he won't shoot 'em but he'll blow a soldier's nose off. Paint a picture of his grandmother's crown that

he won't ever own nobody but when he unowns his own nothing unlike Edward Jones in some unknown world who bought somebody to be different. Simple motherfucker, it's something to be down with how losing and being lost fill up different kind of albums and run over cups. Dance in your head and let go the sped-up real estate like it was in your collar, like in broken rooms to get ready to get ready for my love for you. We live after a river, where me and baby brother found mama, where the rain carried her down from the roof to the foot of her pear tree.

HARRYETTE MULLEN

Bête Noir

Life ain't all beer and skittles
for the white minstrel man
who hums ragtime tunes
and whistles the buckdancer's choice
while he darkens his face
with boneblack
made of human charcoal.

Sometimes, just as he goes onstage,
the holy jimjams grabs him, shakes him loose
from his professional jollification,
and with a giant thumb and forefinger,
holds him dangling
over the dark mouth of the bête noir.

from *Trimmings*

Tender white kid, off-white tan. Snug black leather, second skin. Fits like a love, an utter other uttered. Bag of tricks, slight hand preserved, a dainty. A solid color covers while rubber is protection. Tight is tender, softness cured. Alive and warm, some animal hides. Ghosts wear fingers, delicate wrists.

from *Trimmings*

Her feathers, her pages. She ripples in breezes. Rim and fringe are hers. Who fancies frills. Whose finery is a summer frock, light in the wind, riffling her pages, lifting her skirt, peeking at edges. The wind blows her words away. Who can hear her voice, so soft, every ruffle made smooth. Gathering her fluttered pages, her feathers, her wings.

from *Trimmings*

Her ribbon, her slender is ribbon when to occupy her
hands a purse is soft. Wondering where to hang the keys
the moon is manicured. Her paper parasol and open fan
become her multiplication of a rib which is connected and
might start a fire for cooking. Who desires crisp vegetables,
she opens for the climate. A tomato isn't hard. It splits in
heat, easy. It's seasonal. Once in a while there is heat, and
several flowers are perennials.   Roses shining with green-
gold leaves and bright threads. Some threads do wilt after
starching. She has done the starching and the bleaching.
She has pink too and owns earrings. Would never be
shamed by pearls. A subtle blush communicates much.
White peeks out, an eyelet in a storm.

from *S*PeRM**K*T*

Just add water. That homespun incantation activates potent powders, alchemical concentrates, jars and boxes of abracadabra. Bottled water works trickling down a rainy day watering can reconstitute the shrinking dollar. A greenback garnered from a tree. At two bucks, one tender legal portrait of Saint No-Nicks stands in for clean-shaven, defunct cherry chopper. Check out this week's seasonal electric reindeer *luz de vela* Virgin Mary mark downs. Choose from ten brands clearly miracle H-2-O. Pure genius in a bottle. Not municipal precipitate you pay to tap, but dear rain fresh capped at spring. Cleaner than North Pole snow or Commander in Chief's hard-boiled white collars. Purer than pale saint's flow of holy beard or drops distilled from sterile virgin tears.

from S*PeRM**K*T

A daughter turned against the grain refuses your gleanings, denies your milk, soggy absorbency she abhors. Chokes on your words when asked about love. Never would swallow the husks you're allowed. Not a spoonful gets down what you see of her now. Crisp image from disciplined form. Torn hostage ripening out of hand. Boxtop trophy of war, brings to the table a regimen from hell. At breakfast shuts out all nurturant murmurs. Holds against you the eating for two. Why brag of pain a body can't remember? You pretend once again she's not lost forever.

from *S*PeRM**K*T*

Off the pig, ya dig! He squeals, grease the sucker. Hack that
fatback, pour the pork. Pig out, rib the fellas. Ham it up, hype
the tripe. Save your bacon, bring home some. Sweet dreams
pigmeat. Pork belly futures, larded accounts, hog heaven. Little
piggish to market. Tub of guts hog wilding. A pig of yourself,
high on swine, cries all the way home. Streak a lean gets away
cleaner than Safeway chitlings. That's all, folks.

from *S*PeRM**K*T*

Flies in buttermilk. What a fellowship. That's why white milk makes yellow butter. Homo means the same. A woman is different. Cream always rises over spilt milk. Muscle men drink it all in. Awesome teeth and wholesale bones. Our cows are well adjusted. The lost family album keeps saying cheese. Speed readers skim the white space of this galaxy.

from *Muse and Drudge*

dressed as a priestess
she who carries water
mirrors mojo breasts
Yemoja's daughter

some loose orisha gathering
where blue meets blue,
walk out to that horizon
tie her sash around you

how many heads of cowries
openmouthed oracles
drinking her bathwater
quench a craving for knowledge

kumbla of red feathers
tongues chant song
may she carry it well
and put it all down

tom-tom can't catch
a green cabin
ginger hebben as
ancestor dances in Ashanti

history written with whitening
darkened reels and jigs
perform a mix of wiggle
slouch fright and essence of enigma

a tanned Miss Ann startles
as the slaver screen's
queen of denial a bottle
brown as toast Egyptian

today's dread would awe
Topsy undead her missionary
exposition in what Liberia
could she find freedom to study her story

up from slobbery
hip hyperbole
the soles of black feet
beat down back streets

a Yankee porkchop
for your knife and fork
your fill of freedom
in Philmeyork

never trouble rupture
urban space fluctuates
gentrify the infrastructure
feel up vacant spades

no moors steady whores
studs warn no mares
blurred rubble slew of vowels
stutter war no more

get off your rusty dusty
give the booty a rest
you must be more than just musty
unless you're abundantly blessed

I can't dance don't chance it
if anyone asks I wasn't present
see I wear old wrinkles
so please don't press me

my head ain't fried
just fresh rough dried
ain't got to cook
nor iron it either

you've seen the museum of famous hats
where hot comb was an artifact
now it's known that we use mum or numb our stresses
sometimes forget to fret about our tresses

heard about that gal
in Kansas City got meatballs
yes you shall have cake and eat
your poundcake on the wall

quickie brick houses
don't roll rickrack stones
or bats eyelashes rocks you
till bric-a-brac's got no home

ain't had chick to chirp nor child to talk
not pot to piss in, no dram to drink
get my hands on money marbles and chalk
I'll squeeze till eagle grin, till pyramid wink

tussy-mussy mufti
hefty duty rufty-tufty
flub dub terra incog
mulched hearts agog

hooked on phonemes imbued with exhuberance
our spokeswoman listened for lines
heard tokens of quotidian
corralled in ludic routines

slumming umbra alums
lost some of their parts
getting a start
in the department of far art

monkey's significant uncle
blond as a bat
took off beat path
through tensile jungle

dark work and hard
though any mule can
knock down the barn
what we do best requires finesse

Denigration

Did we surprise our teachers who had niggling doubts about the picayune brains of small black children who reminded them of clean pickaninnies on a box of laundry soap? How muddy is the Mississippi compared to the third-longest river of the darkest continent? In the land of the Ibo, the Hausa, and the Yoruba, what is the price per barrel of nigresecence? Though slaves, who were wealth, survived on niggardly provisions, should inheritors of wealth fault the poor enigma for lacking a dictionary? Does the mayor demand a recount of every bullet or does city hall simply neglect the black alderman's district? If I disagree with your beliefs, do you chalk it up to my negligible powers of discrimination, supposing I'm just trifling and not worth considering? Does my niggling concern with trivial matters negate my ability to negotiate in good faith? Though Maroons, who were unruly Africans, not loose horses or lazy sailors, were called renegades in Spanish, will I turn any blacker if I renege on this deal?

Free Radicals

She brought the radish for the horses, but not a bouquet for
Mother's Day. She brought the salad to order with an unleav-
ened joke. Let us dive in and turn up green in search of our
roots. She sang the union maid with a lefty longshoreman. They
all sang rusty freedom songs, once so many tongues were loos-
ened. She went to bed sober as always, without a drop of wine.
She was invited to judge a spectacle. They were a prickly pair in
a restaurant of two-way mirrors with rooms for interrogation.
The waiter who brought a flaming dessert turned the heat from
bickering to banter. She braked for jerk chicken on her way to
meet the patron saint of liposuction. His face was cut from the
sunflower scene, as he was stuffing it with cheesecake. Mean-
while, she slurped her soup alone at the counter before the gig.
Browsers can picture his uncensored bagel rolling around in
cyberspace. His half-baked metaphor with her scrambled ego.
They make examples of intellectuals who don't appreciate
property. She can't just trash the family-style menu or order by
icon. Now she's making *kimchee* for the museum that preserved
her history in a jar of pickled pig feet. They'd fix her oral trad-
ition or she'd trade her oral fixation. Geechees are rice eaters.
It's good to get a rice cooker if you cook a lot of rice. Please
steam these shellfish at your own risk. Your mother eats blue-
green algae to rid the body of free radicals.

The Lunar Lutheran

In chapels of opals and spice, O Pisces pal, your social pep makes you a friend to all Episcopals. Brush off lint, gentile, but it's not intelligent to beshrew the faith of Hebrews. I heard this from a goy who taught yoga in the home of Goya. His Buddhist robe hid this budding D bust in this B movie dud. If Ryan bites a rep, a Presbyterian is best in prayer. Oh tears oxen trod! To catch oil, or a man born to the manor, you need a Catholic, Roman. On Mon. morn, mom hums "Om" with no other man but Norm or Ron. A Mormon son would gladly leave a gas slave in Las Vegas for a hut in Utah. These slums I'm from I'm leaving, Miss Lum, with a slim sum donated by some Muslims. What would it cost to gain the soul of an agnostic? Where the atheist is at, God only knows! 'Tis hate, he is at the heist. A Baptist was able to stab a pit bull when the sun hid behind some Hindus. To fan a mess, I write manifestos. So said the lunar Lutheran.

Ted Joans at the Café Bizarre

cairo man
surly realist
dis member ship
jungle blackboards
cryptic script
stirring up
dead alive
tongues tired
tarred wool
manifesto folded
unclear arms
cracking open
ivory trunk
of brazil nuts
voodoo toenails
konker root
jockey cornsilk
purrs natch
contraband leader
scattering scat
sporadically all over
forever diaspora

Zen Acorn

for Bob Kaufman

a frozen
indian acorn

a frozen
indiana corn

afro zen
indian acorn

afro zen
indiana corn

a zen fro
in diana corn

frozen fan
in zero canadian

indian corn for
arizona nonradiance

a narco dozen
faze an african

MENDI LEWIS OBADIKE

Determined Invisibility

I sat at our Thanksgiving Day table listening
to my daughter talk about the university and
the horrors of determined invisibility. Over
the years I have recorded her dreams of
death at their hands, **sometimes** glorious,
sometimes cheap. She tells me of the
teachers who refuse to understand simple
questions, who **look** at her as if she were a
benign – meaning **powerless – but** unsightly
tumor. She weeps. I hold her. I tell her to
remember the university doesn't own her,
that she has a home. But I have to let her go
into that jungle of ghosts, having taught her
only how to be fleet of foot, how **to** whistle,
how to love, and how not to **run.** Unless she
has to. It is never enough.

*a poem after Audre Lorde and her "Eye to Eye: Black Women, Hatred, and Anger,"
to be read silently

Tengo, vamos a ver, lo que tenía que tener. – Nicolás Guillén

What I Had to Have

on Giuliani, on Guillén
As with a belief or palmed head: held. Tenet.
Tenant. Not even a small room. Tangible.
Tenebrous. I have, let'see, a having way.
Addiction, you could say. Tendency, you could say.
Habit. Habitat, as in a threshold. Tender. Tenacious.
What I had to have: tenable.

Gassed

Nineteen ninety two. May one. Lungs, first
tested in Palo Alto, fail me
in Atlanta. This breath may be my
last, Ron and Shirley. Daisies bloom and
crush like this. Who can outrun tear gas?
Blue, the clear sky. Blue, their uniforms.

Open

Open is (Her trace of mourning into wrinkled sheets.
Her voice, pronouncing love, her sister's name, loss.
Space behind my tongue, salty and gaping.

I want to say, "I'm sorry."
[I won't. I know it would make her regret her
Open.] A wound.

Open can be a color between pink and brown, the color her lips
Are in this light. Looking at them now, I forget she is happy
now and then.
Think to cradle her, exchange my skin for what it protects.

I need to match her open. So she doesn't stand there,
Being watched. Tell her something
So she sees me) raw.

G. E. PATTERSON

Hesitation Step

"It looks like the surface . . . ."
　　　　　　　—Mei-Mei Berssenbrugge

　　　　". . . falling away from the world . . . ."
　　　　　　　　　　　—Joshua Clover

Hesitation Step:
　　　　". . . the terror and the hungering . . . ."
　　　　　　　　　　　—June Jordan

　". . . this pair of rings . . . ."
　　　　　　　—Marina Tsvetaeva
　　　　　　　(tr. Catherine Ciepiela)

　　　　　". . . only an hour away . . . ."
　　　　　　　　　　　—Henry James

Of course now such seems of looseness of *un-*
We might have left to discover the world
tethering: the heavy blackish shoes worn
When it's raining we want to reach the ground

To satisfy a need someone could imagine
Earlier having had the happy life
Like that man in the store discounting feelings
You bring yourself toward the smiles of cashiers

Once as we've begun to speak of before
We had no idea a cloud could stop
Being battened on the treetops so quickly
It reduced the distance that you can see
Between the different places on a map
Not for our one time but still under it

As If That Alone

"...odd...."
            —Emily Dickinson

                            "... a man...."
                                    —Ralph Waldo Emerson

As If That Alone

                    "...the thing intended...."
                                    —Lyn Hejinian

            Seed (and) Flower

It is not now as in old days he said
Calling out to the Boy the Bight the One
It is not now what they teach and repeat
As he is to us what he is to us

We do not say leave what he is to us
What he is to us the clock has not stopped
We do not say leave so we can see now
What he is to us he is to us what

Weak in judgment still still beneath the sun
It is not now we know that at least
We do not say so so let it be now
He is still to us what he is to us

What he is to us when he turns to us

Is a face pitiless and long delayed

JULIE EZELLE PATTON

> Through the haze I see
> 1,000 crosses
> scratched in the
> —Jimi Hendrix

When the Saints Go

When The Saints Go...   *for the late great Lori June Patton (1959-1991)*
(draw your own conclusions)

CALL (space...

ella FITs angel
kARMa's best RAy
　　bill
li'l alARM sounds
blue MINd GUSts
　　　ScARe A vow
devil o divine hodge
POW! yEll
　　ing tunes
GuSH WINd's COLd bORdER
　　　pres HINT'n JAke-BLAKE
DrIZZlebELl bLaSt-saint
thank 'EaVeN's
TOOT sassy brass
gJILL noise
BOp mouf cAN-
　　　ON lawd altaR LEad
(not utterly i) AM.. n
　　strument of ...od be gottXen
HyMn fILLed LUNg fORced pullit
　　　bud
　　[minnie]　　ha ha　　　hi de ho
　　　ping ear a chord choir key
vESpER YOUNG lILLy HOLy DAYS CRISS croSS
FLEsh CHuRcH miNistERs RICHest w/rite:
St.
RAY horn BlOWIng
MeRrY bLUe WheeL BEe dECK'd PETty FORD
JAck'd up) CAR/d deal Lord,
　　　Duke, King (tokin to d' bridge RUSH
HeARTs spADEs clubs roomy BoLD WINgs
CLIFF DJANglin' roma/n mantric yell
　　ow jacket set author seek
gypsy CAB CALL a kab/allah je
　　hova high hat mass CHanT STANd
h/ard loneLY TOURING TImEs ROYal uba-base
COUNT dis impress BleSS'd MyTH PAST
　　　ORaL (NICkLe-less) bro's perish
salon SuNNY STInt By a YARD: 10th & B square
round gig-mad mean Knights
chilly park air—hawk!
weather vain smiles
cold terrain fur
holiest monk
webstrung halo
sphere ritual
pork pious, dance bias
sleepy Job woe 'ligion
jam sesshin canfusion dishes
every gown's song bird din
　　　ah served (jim crow) mmm!union
host: tooth-sutra FLAme aGAiNst
jazzuit faint BAKER's burnt
offering thATCH MOoch ham mad creedo
JELLY ROLL taffy duck bugs bunny FRANK
friars fast
ether ——————————————

RESPONSE (time...

melodious thunk
rare orb garnets
dark angelic tongue
　　　dub
el lip-scats herald, seraphim
Osiris tao fang, a tad dim
sun-ratarry jewel heart
tea garden Set, Horus silver Ptah pick
genie-hand rich gem stoned fan
tantric bar dose — a fifth of chakra
t' bet peace martyr sufi yah hindu song
oboe tabala sha ma Nile vedas
leave it to divas air witch cloud fount
tear amid ark totem tide Dharma rain neo
hoo brew native
(sammy davis)
kinte conkgOgun Ishstar fun
　　　　key jazZaZen DoJo "jones"
high doll idol arch purr pose
red satin or satan—
"Scratch" phat cat nirvana
apostle chambers
psalm airy weights
songstorm huge:
part sunny
cold rain
sus...tained note
dexterioso
bodyhandsolo
chord on brown
messy mists
hear whine hum &
choke—cold
turkey pope tart poise
sin seine-scene deep bishop
a3hE' head
roll & quit
dense charts
sad hit sticks (sanskit)
busy soul 'lets blow eterni...
　　　tty-gritty
stoney sit strong
arm cheering dawn
pullin' purple
haze tongue awe
smelt lock jaw om kora/n
bible hex times
moon ra & shine
hell merits
all but liars
runny solace
gets up
miles high
g/Lori June
river Jordance
ellalujah!
——————waters

Revelation

REVELATION:	NOTES:
here is the patience of the saints...	a love supreme
pure gold...	
waxed rich...	" " "
set in heaven...	
& their works do follow them...	
Yea...	" " "
ascended...	
cloud thrust...	
every living soul...	" " "
voice of many waters & mighty thunderings...	
withersoever...	
mingled with fire...	" " "
whatsoever...	
garnished with precious stones...	
saints...	" " "
of much people of great tribulation...	
bare record of...	
rest from their labors...	" " "
& the stars of heaven...	
do bring their glory and honor...	
fully ripe...	" " "
art fallen...	
light of harpers & musicians, & of pipers & trumpeters...	
name stand...	" " "
whosoever...	
teeth of lions & the sound of a mil[e]stone...	
(blast fiend)	" " "
which had the trumpet...	
weeping & wailing...	
fountain of the water of life freely...	" " "
gog and magog...	
frogs out of the mouth...	
art holy...	" " "
in the days of the voice of...	
elders sitting clothed in...	
burning...	" " "
wine...	
babble on...	
for they are worthy...	" " "
mouth water...	
on the sea of glass...	
broken to shivers...	" " "
time & time, & half a time, from the face of...	
prophetess JaZz a bell...	
of brass and iron...	" " "
sea & saw...	
poured out...	
fully ripe...	" " "
fill to her double...	
moon to shine...	
voice from heaven...	" " "
smoke of her...	
blow on the earth...	
tongues for pain...	" " "
sing the song...	
art righteous, art, & wast...	
alleluia!	" " "
write, blessed are the dead.	

Notes for Some (Nominally) Awake

"I can see something in the way,

of ourselves

That's why I say the things I do"

ra_m

k a *caw, caw*

Something to *crow*

Bar   a
         k
         a   *boo!*k   (afro turf-truf)

Shhh! Heckle & Jaw-claw
Briar author 1/2 notes: perfect patch blew
Byrds *nommo*

Stuck in your

Que? Que? Que?

"...Bomba, Plena, Salsa, Rain dance, Magical Invective"

To the clannish:

"African, Native American...."
Los Boricuas? A. moor rabble rousing   ba ra ka
                                            ak ar ab

h# Arm *my*riad

Barracks(1954-57)

& the racial mountain (err force)
yet to be dug you

am . . .

I'm

am

am

'nnulphabet-*eye*-kell

em

"Red sp am cans in their throats with the voices..."

400 *y ear* aches & a *moo*!

Jersey
cow
words
transcend

gentile land

*HowL*words (1954)

Paper me
> **Mao** Jones
> jam b or
> read: L rage
> bird sings

B-side:
> party favors ad
> mire
> bro rapper
> buck
> raw courage,

> Font key
> G, I

"Jones" brown
> (joke text)

I am bit **Marx**
> *Get down*
> tongue!

> **"...locked up**
> **in the brig for**
> **wearing zoot suit"**

> *fatigues*
> levee joins no more

→ **ire** *our*
> **aim**

Brer Rare Bit, Chitlin O'

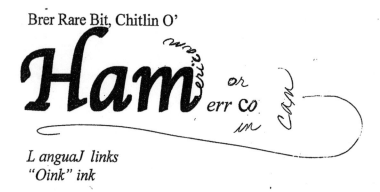

L anguaJ links
"Oink" ink

"Like a newspaper of bleeding meat"

Am i riB, a rack
O
.lamb

Baa Baa black...

Moor than you can
".chew"

off de pigs!

smoke

Sign **L**
read height &
blew **...**

Mind your own buildings

Arf, Arf, Ark

a textural firm
(new gRiot) stories

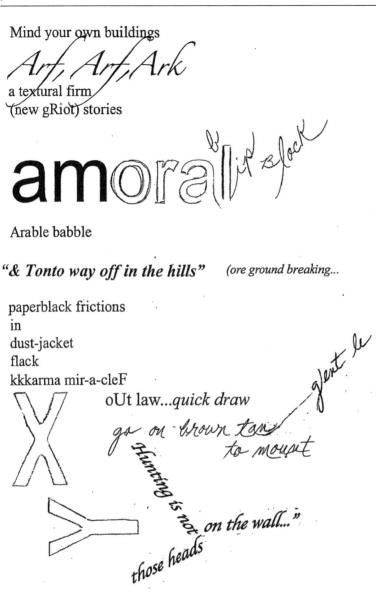

amoral it Black

Arable babble

"& Tonto way off in the hills"   *(ore ground breaking...*

paperblack frictions
in
dust-jacket
flack
kkkarma mir-a-cleF
                        oUt law...*quick draw*

go on brown tan
                    to mount
gent le

those heads
Hunting is not on the wall..."

"Fires were still high as the buildings..."

Lit *towering*   Sun *raw swig*

$$
\begin{array}{ccc}
  & s & o \\
h & t & v \\
a & a & e \\
n & r & r \\
d & s & w \\
s & l & o \\
a & a & r \\
s & v & d \\
s & e & s \\
\end{array}
$$

Amiriborealis

InterSPELLer "OY, aka...A. B. C.rhyme scene
Lone Ranger

Book rocket
A-bomb bard
Rabbi talon like-it-is now
Ark terminal
Kind of blue
Amid a merry *"Oh, B...!*
(1964)

Sirius shouting star comma commies br' royal Pharaoh nuff jazz
Key off a new biz cheops scale *broke em pyre amid sticks & stones...*

*"BoooooolIiiiiiiooooooooooooo...daaaa ahhhhhhh
aaaaahhhhhh...booooooooooooooooooooooooooooooaaaaaaaaaooouaaaa"*

Hip bop s pan Afrikan

no mo-Jo

~~owns~~ <small>(1968)</small>

Book*Rap*

Master *barnacled race*
Slave *deep pens*

Urban New Jersey Visit Bad News For Bear
Associated Press, May 11, 2006

IRVINGTON, N.J.   —A 300-pound black bear that had been wandering around urban New Jersey for two days was shot and killed by police Wednesday in a backyard on the edge of Newark after it reared up on his hind legs and appeared ready to charge.   .

Seven shotgun blasts rang out and the bear slumped to the ground in the small yard where it was cornered.

Before the bear was killed, police chased three or four youngsters from nearby yards, and were becoming increasingly worried that more than 1,000 neighborhood children would soon be walking home from school.

"Why would a bear want to be in Newark?" asked Wanda Williams, upon learning that a **black** bear had been spotted on her street.

"Good gracious! I just hope I don't run into it."

Jim Osorio, an animal control officer said he was ready to fire a tranquilizer shot when the bear assumed an aggressive position. Two officers opened **fire** with shotguns.

"We were going to try to tranquilize the animal and try to relocate him," Osorio said.

"He was jumping over 6-foot fences like they were little curbs."

The bear shooting came only six days after a 225-pound bear was caught in downtown Trenton.

It was shot by state biologists and was the first bear to be killed as part of the state's no-tolerance policy on bears in densely populated areas.

BEar Archer

Higher culling: **"Bee-doo dee bee-doo dee dooo doo"**

State: *Bard Brave Breathwrite Brain Badarf Bam Borough Burnt-Ink-Wand ~~Burstoguen~~ Boldwing Butler Bontemps Brooks Bois Bind Bicker-staff Bookmark Barker Beckett Banshee Biko Bop Bumpers Betshebazz Blackanoir Blaspheremonk Barbecue Bop Belltrain Barracoon Blood Borschtbelt Berry Boy Bullpit Bongo Bama Bowling Brat Bush Bin Bond Bonecrushing Botherate Bayouconstructor BB Bait-trix Bidwisk Buantonimo Bless-Shiny BallyhooWhoooooooooooandthrough Bro-ham Bank Bailfare Bafflegab Boojie Brass Booohooooooooo Buckeroo Blast Bitch Biblebelt Bat-out-of-hell Boustrophedon Braintwister Baldegrets Buddhahead Beret Bellyup Broadway Bitter Bend BlewArch ~~Bind~~ bOrisha Busy Bay Bee Banimal Beatnik Boogeyman Bradical Bat Bitterroot Bytesize Bruise Bugdead Buyout Bambi BYOB Box Bootylicious Beaver Blue Ball Bunny Bison Boo-Koo Blackfeet Baroque Blowfish Battleax Banter Boogaloo Boar Bull_wo_ᵗʰ Bitterfly Bird Beauty Beef Badger Barf Buttout Bum Body Burp Barnyard Boo-Boo*

"Caca! Caca!...

finger prints every

where

amiri cause

Amerikkklan

c
h
a
i
n

C
a
i
n

gain main

able grab bad **bloods** pooriginal sign jargon of sea go sad aim canaan corps brag dead tales
flag gun muzzle jet bushwhack red scalp fire   canine duck fleet front tear b ond water
boarding kin mock   al le lieu rile lee on lay out cock spite floating carcash
label'd crude awe he brew alley corpse overt raj jaw woof tick oink craw neigh baa me ow
moo ham mad flare plank ak 47 911 tale winds trade souls dying out cloud git mo head
mass 40 acres and a mile high million boot tripe schlep hard spin e do rag gulf moat deep
goat purda eek bait pet oil gut tail be hide shiite mum bible poise arms race burqa stock hide
flank gristle hog bin greasy demo mutt rump stake out foil ram fast hymn hock flash pain
buck weep iamb x joint finger lamb brig apple baste shuckin reservation rib chop meat
salaam pig pout nation injure ungun engine bad news bear plain ooze zoo logical curse a
mine ore mock rogue ear rack eerie trial of tears

Read in d Ark

a *mer* chant!

hmm in new world hum an grind helm hymn nail home
an I mal mum im ma mu am en e my man am mo grim

in	in	in	in
mire	nig	dig	deep
gruns	rants	native	igneous

Ply   Mouth

Ship shapes ahoy   *Rock wild heirs*

CrueL of Thumb

IMPERIAL CLAUSE:

Red   *Lionizing*   *Read*

throne   thrown

keloid **poems**

-------------------- :

bruise **people**

em^b^*race*   <dub voice conscious he X >   sep^a^*rate*
(dual)   (duel)

U*as* A

mirror schmear'r

page **rage**   *in poor **taint***

(off the wall)

race face   *import **tint***

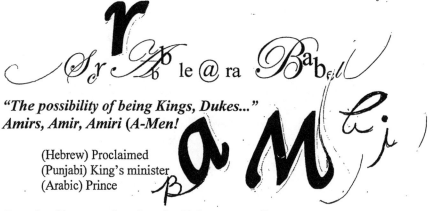

"The possibility of being Kings, Dukes..."
Amirs, Amir, Amiri (A-Men!

    (Hebrew) Proclaimed
    (Punjabi) King's minister
    (Arabic) Prince

Baraka (Ba...ra... key head off the tunes, Count...

    (Arabic) Gracefully bestowed "spiritual energy" or lightening-bolt
    (Swahili) Blessing
    (French) Luck
    (Indonesian) Barakah: favourable gift from Allah or God
    (Hebrew) Berakhah/bracha:Blessing, sense of divine presence, charisma,
    wisdom, "breath of life" *Qi/Prana (Baraqi?)*

    Everette: (German: Eberhard, Courageous as a boar
    Imamu: (Swahili) Spiritual Leader (from Arabic Imam)
    Jones/John: (Hebrew) God is gracious
    Leroy/Leroi: (French) King (*See also Roy, a short form of Royal, Royce*)

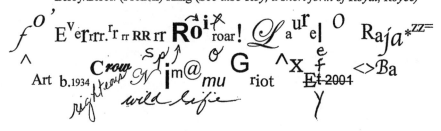

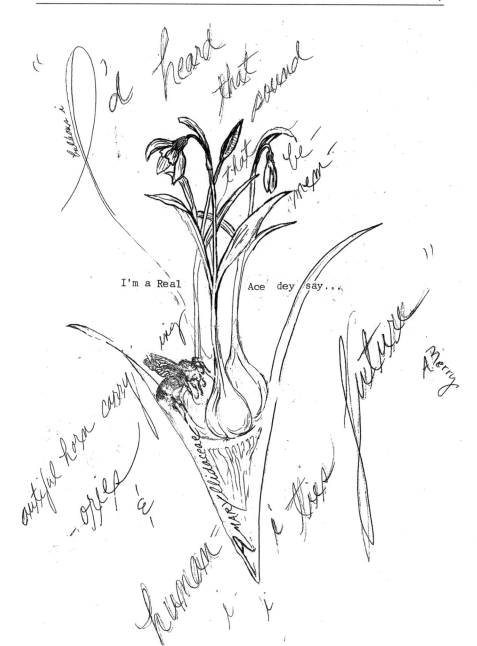

I'm a Real   Ace dey say..

Cam
Air
draw

"Sneaky high up there, pardner…"

Le

"Har to breaf"

War as change sweeps the frame

of breath and meat" meet…

dArk & ᴸove *lies* "Colo**R**ed *colorful color*
color more color color, ahhh..."

black
scarlet

mail
letters

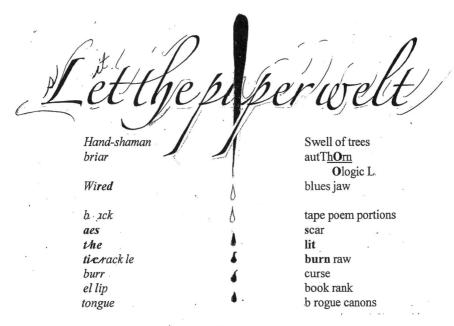

Let the paper welt

Hand-shaman	Swell of trees
briar	autTh**O**rn
	Ologic L.
Wired	blues jaw
b . ick	tape poem portions
aes	scar
the	**lit**
ti crack le	**burn** raw
burr	curse
el lip	book rank
tongue	b rogue canons

"Pick me apart and take the useful parts, the sweet meat of my feelings"

Make no bones	birth of the cruel (kinky
A	rag e on he-role shades
B out it	dun bar hues
Add mired	flame ink
home	eros run
play by play	buss breaking beak

her↓ she Kisses him↓ he (then...

"What will be the sacred words?

Ka
Ba

Scream *e*v *"Honk*

walk a **+**
diss

card stock	paper bararag man
intails	arabesque
alpha	beak
singrr…	fingers
bluesful	ink "even
o	
o	
d	

s **carmine** fades sooner than **black as the**
Legend shows:
Billhornblueclausereadeyeswritewingtipbeatblacktalonsbrokentarsus
gimmick sum **skin**

Bird Racket   Ka Dish

arf

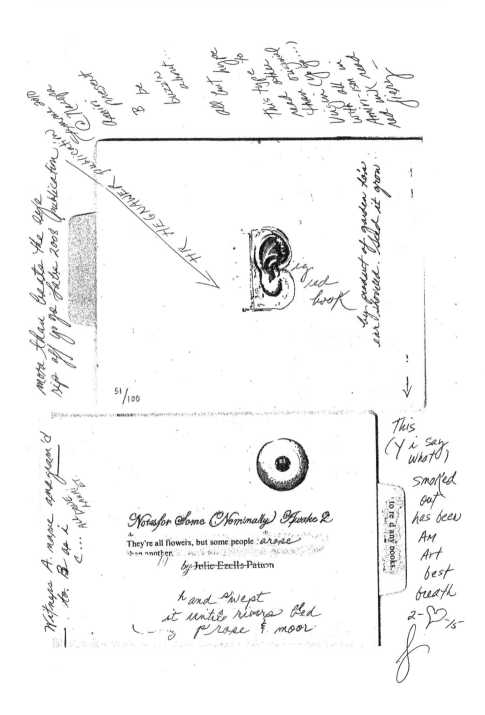

CLAUDIA RANKINE

from Residual in the Hour

One day it is *happy birthday* or *I love you* or *did you know?*
The next day, the next minute,
the ceiling is falling or calling her name or whispering,
rinse your face of this, whispering, *be your own–*

Funny, isn't it?

lying on the ground too ironic to call for help.

from Hunger to the Table

A turned ankle is its own consequence. She hops about,
then caught on the sofa waiting for the swelling to go down
is reminded we move among others to fall from ourselves,
windswept, having a liking for laughter   but
the ridiculousness of falling off one's own heels. What
was being viewed from up there? The mind varies so,
then the tripping up; for the foot, not steadiness, is
at the same time as the mind running about in downpour.
Outside the bathroom, moments before, having just
pulled her panty and his underpants out from where
the lump detracted from tightly tucked bedsheets, she,
in that place which proves as she holds in her hands
the closest mingling of them, scent sweetly wading across
the mouth of love, comes about in this remembering
and is reminded, the ankle throbbing, lying there. And so,
knowing again remarkably, *after all, you*, she, finding
the glass of water between the legs of the sofa, is moved to
respond like any woman collecting rainwater to stay alive.

from Hunger to the Table

Nearer the open hydrants of summer to arrive flung, sung, sweat
stains tossed aside: all effort
past forgotten:
tension of whether forgiven
as the unclothed if disciplined body releases as it wraps its
legs around: closure rewarding and sustained and thigh-high.

Don't ask to be told x to y in time or eternity.
Passage bleeds between the hammering
breaths and flesh. Sweetness mumbled
is the voice nice. Just as the lips open the eyes.

from Toward Biography

as if anguishing could be excrement:
a flabby stink unbandaged
left out overnight:

as if anguishing should be
seeping intrusion hacked into:

as if anguishing:

Liv's View of Landscape I

By landscape we also mean memory–the swept under.
covered over. skin of history. surfacing blue violence of
true. echoing from there. to here.

the depths absorbed to surface. barring the busyness of
flow. urging us toward our cravings. our mouthfuls
crashing over lips.

as our pulled-down soul glances itself as not solved
for. though rimming to fill gaps fetching forward.

I am all of me feeling I am in constant paraphrase.
loosely. without the fence of time. in time losing to form
absorbed. swiftly caught

by my own resistance to the completed sacrifice to
the long line arriving me. bringing everything I mean.
unmistakably personal. to this same feeling of loss. lost

far from here though I am here aiming. though every
plot has prodded. each driven drama digested by this

world. a dawning giving back so much to the self. in
reflection darkening so much. the day might call it night.

Interpretive Commentary

I see you no matter who, says the cloud.

And Liv, still pregnant, having inherited enjambic surprise while knowing what hangs on is never enough, need not be mediated though the struggle in plot against plot lands unsteadily with everything and more is needed. The shape she takes embraces her steadiness thereof, and yet, and frail? and less?

The doggy shouts,

What counts? I see what matters, matters of . . . yes, matters me.

Shellfish. No . . . approach it. Selfish. Oui.

Knock. Knock.
Who's there?
Who cannot be.
Who cannot be who?
Who cannot be known beforehand, fool.

from *Don't Let Me Be Lonely*

I leave the television on all the time. It faces the empty bed. I don't go into the bedroom during the day once I've dressed. Sometimes when I am wearing a skirt and feel like putting on pants or vice versa, I go in there and people are conversing. Occasionally I sit on the edge of the bed and listen. I listen for a few minutes only. One day there is a man interviewing a boy caught in the penal system, a juvenile offender–

Man: He is deceased?
Boy : He is dead to me.
Man: So he is not deceased?
Boy : I don't know.
        He could be dead.
Man: Is he or is he not dead?
Boy : He's been dead to my life.
Man: Someone wrote in your file
        that he is dead. Did you tell
        someone he is dead?
Boy : All right, he is dead.

umm pa pa

That day I find I can't work, so in the margin of my
notebook I write a dialogue.

>
> I thought I was dead.
>
> You thought you were dead?
>
> I thought I was.
>
> Did you feel dead?
>
> I said, God rest me.
>
> God rest your soul?
>
> I thought I was dead.
>
> You tried everything?
>
> I waited.
>
> You spoke aloud?
>
> I said, God rest me.
>
> You'd let me be lonely?
>
> I thought I was dead.

Or say a friend develops Alzheimer's. For a while he understands he is getting ill and will die within this illness. On a slate message board in his house, he writes

He is moved to a home: Manor Care. Then he becomes violent and is moved to another home: Fairlawn. All this takes five years. Then he dies. I bring the chalkboard home with me and hang it on the wall in my study. Whenever I look up from my desk it is there–

One day I hear, as if he is standing next to me, the poet Joseph Brodsky saying, *What's the point of forgetting if it's followed by dying?* Joseph Brodsky is dead, but this fact does not stop his voice from entering the room every time I look up–this is the most miserable in my life *what's the point of forgetting if it's followed by dying* this is the most miserable in my life *what's the point . . .* I can't stop people from saying what they need to say. I don't know how to stop repetitions like these.

The chalkboard has a built-in ledge, on the ledge is an eraser, but he scratched in the words

with some sort of sharp edge.

When his memory started to go he substituted a kind of makeshift reality. He developed the irritation of a three-year-old fighting his way to a sentence. One day he pointed to the television and with great effort and concentration finally said, I want to see the lady who deals in death. The first time you hear him say this, you think his condition has given him insight into his own mortality. The phrase echoes in your head, The lady who deals in death. The lady who deals in death. The lady who deals in death. The lady who deals. Until, finally, *Murder, She Wrote.*

from *Don't Let Me Be Lonely*

I forget things too. It makes me sad. Or it makes me the saddest. The sadness is not really about George W. or our American optimism; the sadness lives in the recognition that a life can not matter. Or, as there are billions of lives, my sadness is alive alongside the recognition that billions of lives never mattered. I write this without breaking my heart, without bursting into anything. Perhaps this is the real source of my sadness. Or, perhaps, Emily Dickinson, my love, hope was never a thing with feathers. I don't know, I just find when the news comes on I switch the channel. This new tendency might be indicative of a deepening personality flaw: IMH, The Inability to Maintain Hope, which translates into no innate trust in the supreme laws that govern us. Cornel West says this is what is wrong with black people today–too nihilistic. Too scarred by hope to hope, too experienced to experience, too close to dead is what I think.

from *Don't Let Me Be Lonely*

The Sunday I turn forty the delivery guy pulls the
front door shut as I pick up the phone to call my parents
and thank them for the lilies. "A lovely flower. I
carried them on my (birth) day and now I place them
in this vase in memory of something that has died,"
Katharine Hepburn in *Stage Door*. My parents' house-keeper
answers the phone.

May I speak to my mother?

They're still at the funeral.

Whose funeral?

Is everyone you know alive?

DEBORAH RICHARDS

Parable

then there was a film on tv   about a good time girl   in the
forties   of course it was black and white   well   this girl goes
to a psychiatrist because she's been having too much fun   with
a different lad   each good time   she drinks   laughs
and enjoys herself   so much   that she has a reputation
but something happens   and she wants to give them up
those good times

******

it was the night   she fled the millionaire's grasp   then tried to
run her car off the bridge   that was when she met the psychiatrist
who happened to be passing by   that was fortunate

******

well   they thought she'd killed the millionaire   not then   that
time in his mansion before she dashed her car into a   ditch
but later   when she'd met a nice man willing to marry her
well this man had fallen in love with her illusion   not knowing
it was   you see it came up in court   the millionaire had been
to her room that evening   he   the fiancé   had proposed
and she'd accepted the proposition   they should make their life
together   I suppose that would mean relocation   her
plans are always adaptable

******

so the boyfriend is mad   his emotion registers in the close up
well   he's not really mad but shocked   the psychiatrist had said
she   was   escaping   her   problems   by   considering   the   nice guy
so tell him your sordid past   that's the least you should do
but the past came up in court before she could   the fiancé
disgusted   says to the psychiatrist   what's this got to do
with me   she was my fiancé   so who are these men who
want to make love to her   and in those days   making love
meant something else   maybe kissing   in the french style
and while the woman bends backwards   you can see her pure
white neck   open and vulnerable   her eyes close if
she is   really   in love   her eyes open if she is thinking
or plotting something

******

the woman is on trial   for a murder she did not commit   she
would rather be tried   found guilty then hanged   because
that man doesn't love her anymore   her counsel pleads   but
she doesn't say a word in her defense   she has the beautiful
wickedness   of a fallen woman   then the boyfriend starts
to think scientifically   he follows the loose ends   through the
maze of circumstance   then I was thinking about these
stories   the woman needing the love of a scientific man   who
can rescue her from the kind of freedom that makes her drive
her car off the road   and or   jump from a bridge

******

and this man should love her even   if he finds out that another
man   has been making her neck bend back   while he's at a
conference   presenting the paper she has illustrated
when his supervisor sees his research   he says   I hope your
paper is as good as the illustrations   and he   the fiancé doesn't
admit that she drew them   but she doesn't mind   in fact she
smiles grabs his arm   and they go to have dinner   we don't
see what they eat

******

when she is acquitted   she writes the fiancé to thank him   and
to say   she's going away for a while   with the idea of further
improvement   if he still wants her yes   they can start again it's
all very touching and penitent   but it might have been a ploy
she could have been bored as a doctor's gal   but didn't want to
hurt his feelings   maybe he really preferred her previous
life of fur coats and early evening cocktails   to her current
existence in peasant blouses with cocoa at bedtime   there's
always something up the sleeve

******

so she's leaving   we don't know where she is going   but it feels
like a long way   the psychiatrist is at the airport   but this time
he thinks she should stay with the scientist   I don't know why
he's convinced   except that   the boyfriend wrestled the
murderer to the ground   telephoned the police on springfield
7 double 2 1   that's not the point but it adds to the plot   of
course her man comes before she gets on the plane   as they do

in all the good films   they kiss on the tarmac   she bends back
her neck so white and intact   he stands above her she
disappears underneath   then it ends   with the psychiatrist's
smile   this is the cure he thinks   because all we really need
is   someone or something   to rely on   and something that
shows   our lives are worth the attention   now she has someone
more important than herself

******

the psychiatrist has gray streaks   and the scientist with broad
shoulders looks like the actor   who played pinky's boyfriend   in
pinky   pinky is not a good time girl   but she wants to be
loved just the same and her off screen lover is that square white
man   she is a black woman   who looks white   and as
she is played by a white actress she really looks the part   the
boyfriend   perhaps this same actor   is a doctor too   he comes
down and finds   that pinky is living in a shack with her
grandmother played by ethel waters   and everyone can see that
waters is black   in fact   she is known for it in all her films
the   grandmother   thinks   it's a   sin   for pinky to   act
white   so she   hides   the letters that might entice her to turn
back   on duty

******

though the grandmother can't read   she knows by the feel the
letters are important   she doesn't know   they are from the
white doctor   but   she knows that life is hard for pinky even
with her education   and good looks   but in the end it's
better to be with your own kind   that stops a lot of confusion
the doctor turns up because he never gets a reply   and it seems
to me that this actor   if it is the same guy   must have pretty

bad luck with women   because they are never what they
appear   a white looking black woman   a naive
looking siren yet he   that actor   is not a hollow man   his   heart
is full   and his shoulders are set square   he goes to the
courthouse again   in a scene with the dramatic tension of
ceiling fans   but there's no psychiatrist and he doesn't have to
wrestle anyone to the ground   though he takes pinky's arm
guides her out of the courtroom   all the white people look but
say nothing   it's written all over them

******

anyway pinky wins the case   though the town is against a colored
girl inheriting from that rich white woman   you   see   pinky
became the main beneficiary   and her grandmother   waters
witnessed the will with her mark at the right place   the white
people being in charge of the law   were too sure of their
abilities to write the outcome   there is appropriate restitution

******

in the end   the squared doctor wants pinky to leave the shack
and   these people   and go back to being rosemary   or patricia
or something   take up with him again   move somewhere be
someone else   keep herself to himself   identity hidden   a good
deal you'd think   and she doesn't have to think twice
he is slightly shocked in a medium ranged shot   how could she
turn him down he is doing the right thing   when he discovers
her in the black shack   he kisses her   her neck bends back
like a white woman's act   though she is a   stand-in for true
beauty   she is close enough to the real thing   but he never
kisses her again

****

well   he takes his hat and walks out just like that   she holds
onto the door post   watches him leave   but that may not be
true   she could have turned away   closed the door   but
anyway   he leaves she stays   that's an ending   it could have
killed grandmother   if pinky had made tracks back   pinky
acts for her people   setting up a training hospital   for
colored nurses   and a play school   for colored children
the old   lady's house is transformed but it means that   pinky is
never going to marry and have her own colored kids   that
square doctor was her last chance   but she would have been
living a white lie

******

in the other film   the guy gets the gal and she's going all the
way but she is a dark horse   who needs a rider with a good
hand   of   cards   anyway   it is lucky pinky said no   then he
could marry a really white woman   and have really white
children   2 is a good number

******

junior would look like him   be square blond and healthy
and he'd attend the right white schools   and be a doctor like
dad   the girl would reflect his housewife   she'd wear

bows in her hair and her curls would bounce when she ran   to
kiss daddy goodnight   he would smile when her hair bounced
up and down   then he would swing her   around and around
and his really white wife would be marginally under control
and the furniture would be the same place and there wouldn't
be any secrets in dark cupboards   so everything would be as
plain   as the pretty little nose on her face   now that's a
woman who can count her chickens

******

and in these stories   the bad guys   are rounded up before the
end but the actors can't stand still   and move into new locations
before the paint dries on a picket fence   the landlady   in   the
house of the good time girl it's none of my business but it's funny that
you don't go nowhere   you're young etc etc   she has her
hand on her hip or is somewhere assymetrical   it was a short
scene but she made the most of it   she gets the good girl thinking
and by chance an old girlfriend needs her help   because you
don't ring a bell if it doesn't work

******

the girlfriend is curious and says   let's have a little drinkie
like the good old days   before you know it   the good
woman gets drunk   because they give her the usual martini
and as she's been unusually sober she is wobbly   it takes courage
to say no when they're pouring them out   she makes up her
mind to leave before they add up to trouble   she manages to
get up   put on the fur coat   though her arms and legs are out
of control   but when she leaves   she stumbles across that

millionaire   who gives her a ride to his mansion   she
becomes the last person to see him alive   you
know the rest

******

this is my research work on american culture   and the past is
much easier to arrange   I'm a bit   a little bit   like jack
nicholson in the shining   he's a writer who feigns   gets angry
at his wife   for breaking his pretense of busyness   but
that's not the main point   I do housework in place of creativity
but my papers are stacked everywhere   I find my words
on scraps between the pages of magazines   then I start to
read an article I had meant to read before   then halfway
through I think   god   I should be doing something
I look at the long list on the back of another scrap   then I get
crazy   because that's what you say here   so I make tea and
think look how can I work like this   it's impossible   then I
put on the tv and pretend that it's important work   I try but I
know   I'm like those women   that square actor is attracted
to   I get messy at the edges

******

I like to collect the odd thing I trip over   I found a glass
marble last week and I forgot about it until yesterday when   I
put my hand in the pocket of my big fluffy coat   it was a
comfort   maybe I could find a psychiatrist with gray streaks
in her hair   I could confess to things I'd done   or was thinking
of doing   and then they would be off my chest   and I could
stumble on someone   who would kiss me   and bend my neck
back   it would be nice to surrender and be supported   oh
joy   rapture   I would have wonderfully arched eyebrows and

my lipstick wouldn't smear on wine glasses   and I'd wear
swing coats that don't have buttons and shoes with a wedged
heel   and have legs with the right amount of muscle or perhaps
I'd be more active and wear slacks   neat shirts with a cravat
around my throat   and I'd smoke or   have my hands in my
pockets when I stand in hotel lobbies   it would be a class act

                              ******

yet when I get home I'd have to look in the mirror   and get used
to it   and   stop   feeling sorry for not having all those nice attributes
pretty skin   and hair that promises deliverance when you put
your fingers through it   and maybe   my mother could look at
me and think that I didn't let her down too much   I'm too
dark to be beautiful in her circles   and too educated   to
be good company for the boys from back home   who appreciate
a   woman with skills   in very small   small-talk while making
spicy chicken rice   peas and salad   on the side   with avocado
and fried plantain   now my mother wonders   if I will ever
find a husband   even a white one with the right kind of
manners   would be acceptable   even that one I'd been seeing
for all those years   whatever   happened to him   now that
yu 'ave a college heducation   you can sekkle down 'fore   it
get too late uh   uh   but this is not how she speaks   but it might
be a way for communication to begin   if one tongue could be
more truthful than another   but my answers avoid eye contact
I'm a cowardly line in the sand she doesn't step over

                              ******

so I come to america   a great place   to get busy and keep
secrets   because   they don't care what you do as long as

you don't push their faces in it   and secrets can't exist without
a potential audience   if I do it with the light off or with my eyes
closed thinking of something else   does that   make   me   a   little
devious   or am I making do like everyone else   so until I find
my heart's desire   in my own backyard   this is a good place to
avoid thinking

******

my early dream was to be dorothy   I don't think I am the right
kind of woman to be bent backwards   but I would consider a
stay in the emerald city   never return to kansas   show a
clean pair of red heels   and that's the horse of a different
color you heard tell of   but the people wear the same shade
of green

******

dorothy is not a woman   she doesn't see into the future   her
basket is open for all to see   she says what comes into her
mouth   beats up that bully of a lion   then agrees to take him
along   though he seems a liability   she doesn't worry about
makeup and mirrors   except when she goes to see the wizard
and they sing about the merry old land of ha ha ha ho ho ho
then they're off to see the wizard   the wonderful wizard of
oz so it's not a female thing or a scarecrow thing or a tin man
thing   or a lion thing

******

that's what we need   a wizard to believe in   yet in the end
dorothy conforms   keeps her dog under control   stays inside
helps aunty em   then meets a nice squishy farmer who'll
scratch his head wondering what a christian woman would say
after 23 years   and she'll do up the parlor in the spring   and
there will be boys   and girls in scrubbed down overalls   that
she'll darn on the porch at night   and she'll count her chickens
there'll be no promises to be broken   but soon her energy
will dissipate   like silver dust from a wand   because magic
only happens in technicolor   so she won't remember the blue
birds beyond the rainbow   oh   she'll be careworn   and
make a lovely echo when tapped softly   everyone will feel safe
because a woman understands the space between reality and
fantasy

******

in the film you can come to conclusions not found in the book
unless you want it to be a copy   I like the notion of the yellow
brick road   and that little hop skip motion   and the song
and the way the scarecrow's legs buckled after a while and they
had to pull him up by the arm   so they could keep dancing
they were friends who could pep you up   meanwhile
judy was counting calories checking her reality off the screen   but
the studios complained   mickey rooney was a cutey   all
chubby and loveable   and now he's old enough to endorse
life insurance   there are few surprises when you live to his age
judy had an overdose   because she couldn't be anything   but
a sad siren crashing her life on the rocks clink clink she belonged
to them and did what they said until the money ran out   and
the credits rolled on   talent is not enough

******

there's something not quite right about   a   woman that does not
fit in   home is self contained   not all over the place
there is a point   dorothy has to grow up   start with some
silence   increase the spaces between herself and others   divert
her attention if that will help   and watch the grains fall in the
hourglass   is it too much to ask

EVIE SHOCKLEY

art of dakar (or, tourist trap)

> *a senegalese activist reported that trees,*
> *some more than a century old, had been cut*
> *down everywhere the [u.s.] president was*
> *scheduled to pass.*
> —*jonah engle*, the nation, *7/23/2003*

poems are bullshit unless they are trees a century old, sentries lining the streets of senegal. in dakar, the darker brother keeps his peace, while a bush burns in effigy. a poem should show, not tell, so hold up your arms as if they were trees: if you have enough digits to make a fist, you are now a double amputee. terror perches in branches with its sights set on power ties, so no trees on these roots. a poem in jeopardy appeals perversely to the senses. the space where what you haven't seen used to be (*what did these trees look like?*). less traffic on the main thoroughfares (*what did these trees smell like?*). using *like* or *as*, describe the impact of the visit on the city: dakar, comatose quadriplegic, stunned by the thundering walk and big stick of a blowhard. and where are the residents of gorée island, while the resident of a white house tours a red one? come on, concentrate. clean shot photo ops, souvenirs at low low prices. all sales final: no return.

atlantis made easy

orange was the color of her address, then blue silt : : whiskey burned
brown down the street, then a dangerous drink whirled around a paper
umbrella : : intoxication blue across the porch then rose in the attic : :
bloated tuesday taught us, she's never been dry and never will be : : brass,
bass, ivory, skins : : i hate to see that ninth ward wall go down : : army
corpse engineers ran a 'train on her : : aw chere : : sweet ghost, saturated,
deserted : : teething ground for the expected spectre, we knew it'd show up
better late (against a black backdrop), whenever : : wait in the water, wait
in the water, children : : stub your soul on a granite memory, a marble key
change, an indigo mood : : trouble (the water)

henry bibb considers love and livery

The circumstances of my courtship and marriage, I

standing around   flat-footed   love-grounded

no wings no hope   no fleet   vessel   vassal

consider to be among the most remarkable events

star-struck   seeing   dazed   stunned

standing around   constellation   consolation

of my life while a slave. To think that after I had

via stars   whiling   labored   willing

to love   head-first   head-over   heel

determined to carry out the great idea which is so

bound   bounded   headstrong   heady

transported   exported   excess

universally and practically acknowledged among all

one good turn   practice   perfect

cosmos   standing around   seeing

the civilized nations of the earth, that I would be

citizen   vessel   borne   vassal

gaea   terra story   conditional   future perfect free or die, I suffered myself to be turned aside

    to love   *bound*   *to mortify*   *flesh*

liberty   *versus*   *one*   *star-struck*

by the fascinating charms of a female, who gradually

spell   *bound*   *flesh*   *gaea*

    stellar   *light*   *years*   *slow burn*

won my attention from an object so high as that

    suffered   *labored*   *waiting*   *rapt*

love-grounded   *standing around*   *stellar*

of liberty; and an object which I held paramount

free   *flee*   *fleet*   *rapt*

    paramour   *to love*   *manipulate*   *via stars*

to all others.

    against stars

you must walk this lonesome

say hello to moon leads you into trees as thick as folk on easter pews dark but
venture through amazing was blind but now fireflies glittering dangling from
evergreens like christmas oracles soon you meet the riverbank down by the
riverside water bapteases your feet moon bursts back in low yellow swing low
sweet chariot of cheese shines on in the river cup hands and sip what never
saw inside a peace be still mix in your tears moon distills distress like yours
so nobody knows the trouble it causes pull up a log and sit until your empty
is full your straight is wool your death is yule moonshine will do that barter
with you what you got for what you need draw from the river like it is well
with my soul o moon you croon and home you go

a thousand words

torture   torture   torture   torture   torture   torture   torture   torture   torture   torture   torture   torture   torture   torture   torture
torture   torture   torture   torture   torture   torture   torture   torture   torture   torture   torture   torture   torture   torture   torture
torture   family   class   wedding   graduation   prom   panoramic   pornographic   paleoanthropic   yabba   dabba   doo   abu   torture
torture   scream   shout   spill   tell   all   twenty   questions   and   answer   me   bitch   snitch   itch   scratch   and   sniff   whiff   torture
torture   tincture   suture   fe ature   aperture   adventure   puncture   creature   lecture   couture   stature   denture   fracture   torture
torture   dog   man   penis   bars   wars   words   world   premiere   spotlight   light   of   day   night   of   day   right   of   way   away   torture
torture   cat   fight   fright   freight   fraught   taught   t aut   as   a   wire   fire   ready   aim   maim   claim   same   just   the   same   just   torture
torture   halls   walls   prison   freedom   democracy   demonic   evil   eve   apple   of   my   eye   why   so   shy   smile   say   cheese   torture
torture   chamber   bed   pot   maid   made   the   devil   do   it   you   oughta   be   in   sna p   shots   bullets   speeding   needle   torture
torture   bombs   away   you   dropped   the   bomb   on   me   baby   burn   baby   inferno   hell   smell   shit   dung   feces   species   torture
torture   separate   men   from   boys   from   women   from   machines   from   monsters   from   homes   from   families   from   torture
torture   perfect   reflect   genuflect   bow   bough   poplar   trees   strange   fruit   pick   prick   suck   mimic   one   hour   photo   torture
torture   when   the   bough   breaks   stakes   shake   it   like   a   polaroid   window   peek   sneak   look   see   to   shining   sea   torture
torture   flee   beat   it   boo   gie   jungle   desert   tropical   paradise   sandstorm   windstorm   maelstrom   strom   thurmond   torture
torture   flood   flow   leak   drip   drip   drip   drip   chinese   water   lose   my   mind's   eye   visualize   sexualize   lights   camera   torture
torture   bush   shrub   hedge   fence   steal   steel   oil   s   limy   greasy   dirty   black   gold   coast   continent   dark   congo   bonzo   torture
torture   naked   strip   rape   stick   truncheon   luncheon   eat   meat   pork   swine   pig   gas   tear   orange   tea   party   boston   torture
torture   bosnia   ethnic   ethic   thick   tricky   dick   kissinger   killing   fields   cambodia   tuol   sleng   skull   and   crossbones   torture
torture   crossbow   spear   assault   rifle   missile   nuclear   warhead   pothead   smoke   fire   inhale   impale   severed   head   torture
torture   shower   camp   station   ghetto   inner   city   tenement   project   projectile   target   practice   bl ack   brown   beige   torture
torture   life   is   beautiful   stunning   shocking   awful   terrible   terrifying   like   resembling   similar   to   same   as   terrorism   torture
torture   civil   war   civilization   domestication   home   front   lines   infantry   infantile   juvenile   delinquent   detainme nt   torture
torture   jesus   dr.   seuss   lorax   trees   orchards   fields   crops   farm   harvest   migrant   immigrant   border   cross   nailed   torture
torture   holocaust   cost   effective   genocide   genetic   eugenic   gene   jeans   blues   levi   strauss   anthropology   man   kind   torture
torture   to   wer   power   trip   travel   air   fair   just   justice   supreme   court   house   white   might   out   of   sight   incite   riot   pat   torture
torture   yourself   in   a   boat   on   a   river   with   tangerine   trees   and   marmalade   skies   fantasize   escape   flight   addiction   torture
torture   moderate   middl e   center   centerfold   spreadsheet   spread   eagle   with   pornography   for   one   nation   under   torture
torture   united   handcuffed   mangled   martyred   all   saints'   eve   capacity   crowd   halloween   no   room   at   the   inn   torture
torture   hogs   dogs   gods   clash   of   the   titans   atlas   sisyp hus   hades   shades   shadows   closed   doors   self   surveillance   torture
torture   video   panopticon   prisoners   speak   digitally   on   cell   phones   home   teleprompting   images   rosie   is   riveted   torture
torture   woman's   place   is   in   the   house   of   horrors   howling   we   have   met   the   fr ankenstein   monster   and   she   is   us   torture
torture   me   rollin   over   human   rights   gangstah   style   meanwhile   back   at   the   ranch   branding   iron's   on   the   fire   torture
torture   hard   to   define   but   i   known   it   when   i   obscene   it   name   shame   game   sporting   try   survival   of   the   hit - ist   torture
torture   hazing   initiation   you're   in   capitalism   christianity   civilization   wear   the   letters   with   pride   prude   prank   torture
torture   good   clean   fun   for   all   ages   bc   and   ad   bachelor   party   laughs   last   right   through   wedding   day   massacre   torture
to   rture   sand   shit   dirt   dogs   cells   saddam   bush   two   wrongs   make   a   right - wing   financial   fundamentalist   coo(p)   torture
torture   glory   gory   fall(el)ujah   battle   him   beat   him   defeat   him   demoralize   him   demolish   him   desecrate   him   torture
torture   talk   inform   cooperate   jump   down   turn   around   pick   cotton   auction   block   cell   block   black   buck   fucked   torture
torture   all   systems   go   full   speed   ahead   a   ok   roger   thumbs   up   two   thumbs   up   must   see   blockbuster   ballbreaker   torture
torture   cliffhanger   a   thousand   and   one   nights   scheheraz ade   tells   stories   as   if   her   life   depends   on   fictiona - lies   torture
torture   window   frame   view   vista   horizon   her   eyes   on   his   bare   bear   body   lumbering   wood   hard   rod   sodomize   torture
torture   pile   pyramid   stack   stake   raise   ante   anti   muslim   muslin   linen   lenin   len   non   imagine   assassin   ass   mule   torture
torture   painting   panting   heaving   vomit   spit   spew   by   numbers   death   count   toll   bell   horn   porn   viewer   voyeur   torture
torture   sadist   soldier   guard   warden   governor   president   prime   minister   leader   ruler   emperor   master   lord   g od   torture
torture   rack   fire   needles   under   nails   dismemberment   solitary   confinement   threats   to   loved   ones   electroshock   torture
torture   postcard   wish   you   were   here   souvenir   come   again   soon   y'all   come   back   now   ya   hear   ear   fear   dear   dad   torture
torture   dorian   paint   me   a   canvas   capture   reality   humanity   preserve   beastiality   ignorance   evil   illusions   eternal   torture
torture   flesh   ashtray   cheek   boot   cleaner   penis   joystick   prison   playstation   father   dog   thralldom   pyrrhic   victory   torture
torture   telescope   microscope   m agnifying   glass   spectacles   viewfinder   binoculars   closer   closer   try   a   contact   lens   torture
torture   disappeared   vanished   vanquished   vamoosed   vaporized   victimized   vide   invalidated   veni   vidi   vici   torture
torture   we're   losing   our   heads   hoods   masks   lone   ranger   k eeping   the   planet   safe   from   communism   community   torture
torture   your   favorite   foreign   movie   won't   you   smile   for   the   camera   i   know   i'll   love   you   better   i've   seen   your   torture
torture   vogue   rogue   rouge   blush   zinfandel   infidel   intifida   infanticide   insecticide   sect   sectionalism   shun   torture
torture   hooded   bagged   stacked   stripped   wired   leashed   cuffed   smeared   objectified   what's   wrong   with   this   torture
torture   motion   x - ray   perfect   window   book   gallery   frame   puzzle   tube   do   ya   get   the   words   worth   or   worthless   torture
torture   torture   torture   torture   torture   torture   torture   torture   torture   torture   torture   torture   torture   torture   torture
torture   torture   torture   torture   torture   torture   torture   torture   torture   torture   torture   torture   torture   torture   torture

poem   for when his arms open   so wide
you fall through

poem	for when his arms open	so wide	you fall through
a disappointment	a devastation	a disaster	a deviation
	all of the above		at least
(at best)		the first	
		and the last	but perhaps the gift
requires the loss	and that is what		i am waiting to see
		shake the ticking package	wrapped so nicely
i am testing trust	going out on a limb		in the tree
	that just dropped me	because one bad branch	
		don't spoil the whole	
		trunk	
right	a word-worker		has inscribed his name
in my soul	in letters of blood	and the question is	
	whose blood		or how many people's
is it still bleeding			
or simply a red record of	what bled		so many complications
		when did it all	
		get so complicated	i thought it was just
love	and here i was thinking		
	that love is just		trust

aftermath

the aftermath is always there from

the beginning. after all, when she

kissed you, the butter slid off your

knife. the way summer or spring

followed winter was a sign you

couldn't have missed. and the many-

eyed potatoes, you didn't believe

his leg always shook like that,

did you? *did you?* water this part

of the world was supposed to swirl

the other direction. arrows pointed

and shot. stock optioned and

dropped. a funny smell had you

giggling for days. in long final

division, something's always left

over. you could have done the math

before.

a course in canvas

glasper casts an agile shadow : : *left hand step to right hand float* : : runagate pace, *pace* the forgetful : : *left hand do what right hand do* : : playing the changes a century don't make : : *left hand shade while right hand color* : : pulls the 90s up at the roots : : *left hand cradle the right hand blue-bop* : : transplants the tuber into tyner's soil : : *left hand respond to right hand call* : : hip hop head all locks and keys : : *left hand swing and right hand scatter* : : timely, composed in shifty signatures : : *left hand throw what right hand blueing* : : glasper's a hobo riding the rail : : *left hand steal away right hand home*

not in the causal chain

i you she liu they shiites we mericans girls he williams coloreds you

heartbreak loss ignorance fear rage grief desire pride greed despair

redwood him appeal fans family limb mobility savings clique her faith

might possibly ought theoretically **could** *probably would maybe should*

fire hurricane knife needle law penis gun wage tornado tongue wish

lung brain kidney seed motor mind tide memory evolution soul heart

end pass stop decease terminate stop cease transition fail stop quit **die**

GIOVANNI SINGLETON

from melanin suite

1st movement

the study of silence. its evolution a
guard rail. a corrugated

tongue. teeth knitted together. silence
leaves a strain of being work. of looking

almost dead. shade burns as if to
interfere. photographs. a need to hold

still for a moment. everything that
counts appears in past tense. time

accumulates as in a reflecting pool.

2nd movement

stooping in a darkened hallway. salt water
bodies rock steady. muffled pounding. the
door of no return. is closed and closer
and under measured reconstruction. living
seeps through in echoes. stillness outside
in. a collective breath persists without
apology. mud stained spoons undulate from
shore to distant shore. then one day
walk as if rowing a boat.

3ʳᵈ movement

anyone configures everyone at random. long
and short tangents of breath shift then
collide. a departure of selves. memories
and forgetfulness. there in is some predestination. to go on
      and into other
spheres. a rear exit. the route made
visible. singularity of purpose breaks
down in momentum. sleep moves without
sound as in amazing grace.

4th movement

we us and thou. the voices. sound a
decidedly downtown destination. the

boulevard. blazing speech. horns blow.
fast and furious. ghostly

drummer makes flight. some rap

tap   tap   tap   tap   tap

conductor of multi-directional live-
wire. crowds gather

behind cranial walls. all smoke-filled.
goat praises. thou. a vast expanse of

skeletal remains. faced down on the
ground as in quilted covering.

5th movement

spinning wheel fortune, stagger the root. warrior

rifts. a cataclysmic sight. mythical weave of bowed

heads. discontinuous dreams and drafts. drawing

hands. acoustic bass. plucked upright. mercurial

conjure. strings. such tongues ever

leaning as in revelation.

AMERICAN LETTERS

EXHIBIT A
American Prose

```
                              [PS508.N3c66]
                              [PZ4.K285De]
                              [PZ4.J7553]

[PR9320.9.H3C3][PS153.N5M24][PS3563.A3166D53]
  [PZ3.D3923BE5][PR9320.9.H3R47][PZ4.M652Fr]
   [PZ4.R82254Or][PS3555.V34G6][PZ4.H318As]
      [PS3563.A39A45][PS3562.0442L5]

[PS3563.A3166B4][PS3561.E392D5]
[PS3560.0483M67][PS3555.V34Z8]
[PZ4.57276Le][PZ4.M23A][PS3553.A7736...]
```

EXHIBIT B
American Poetry

[PR9272.9.C54D6][PS3529.D44T5]
[PS3573.E14M3][PS3562.A378L5]
[PS3570.H568B3][PS3563.U3954T75]
[PS3566.R58E3][PS3569.0765M3]
[PS3558.U46766A89][PS3553.072S25]
[PS3573.R5364D4][PS3573.R5364H6]
[PS3561.E423T5][PS3570.H568C5]
[PS3566.R58A6][PS3557.I78H47]
[PS3553.072C6][PS3573.R5364A6]
[PR9230.9.B68M54][PS3568.0235J8]

[PR6052.R29R5][PS3561.A84G6][PS3563.C3872B53][PS3557.I78G57][PS3557.I78H47][PS3563.0235E8][PS3568.0235E8]

[PS3568.0235W5][PS3568.0235J8][PR9230.9.B68A6][PR9230.9.B68B5][PS3552.A583A17][PS3552.A583R4][PS3560.076A63][PS3562.04418J8][PS3554.U43P6][PS3551.T55H4][PS3558.U46766L6][PS3568.0235E8]

EXHIBIT   C
American Letters

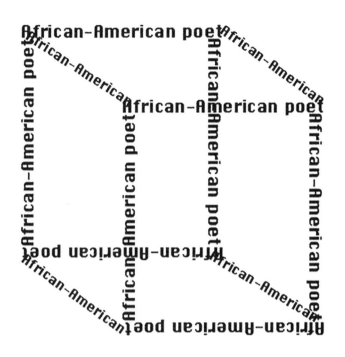

Fig. 1

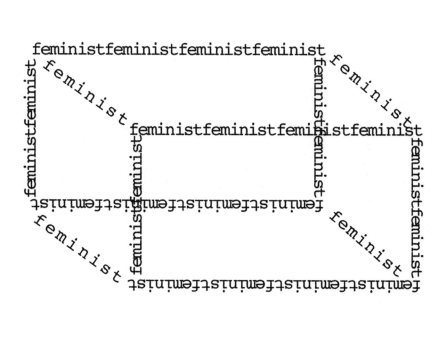

Fig. 2

Fig. 3

Fig. 4

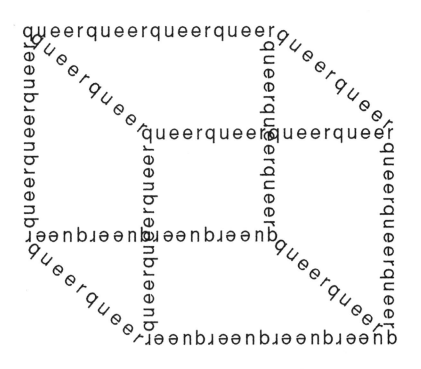

Fig. 5

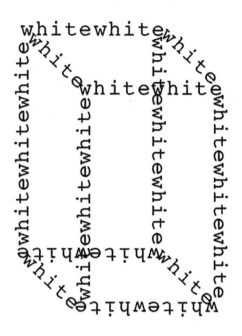

Fig. 6

from Atias: The Green Book

Scene 8. a lesson before kissing

In a french novel, a zookeeper falls in love with a giraffe. Some time later, he catches her with another giraffe. This illicit affair awakens him to the realization that he would never be able to fully please the tall spotted beauty whose long eyelashes had often caressed his face. Because of his love for her, he decides that in fact he will have to do away with her. Afterwards, the zookeeper donates the giraffe's skeleton to the museum of Natural History. And although her betrayal continues to plague him, he goes to the museum every day, climbs a ladder, and wipes the dust from her eyes.

mesostic for Ree Dragonette

staRfall of
kinEtic dust
nova sEx elegy say

ontological inDifference
tRee-rock of
hyAcinth
finGers steeped in
cObalt glue
quaNtum of
modus vivEndi
sTicks vaporous speech
inTo
John C.'s Encyclical eyelids

mesostic for the Sun Ra Arkestra

aStro black
proUd
fiNs, flesh

and cRown
subliminAlly

trAnsmit
puRple
peeKaboo
interstEllar
chantS
faiThfully
thRough
mAitreyan verse

mesostic: *Golden Sardine*
(after Bob Kaufman)

amonG

terra cOtta

riddLles

anD a

flutEd

visioN

bliSter

mAdness

colouRs the

sounD of

a nIght poet's

boomeraNg

voyagE

the odds

read the leaves roll the dice shuffle the cards lay the runes write some poems and pray pray pray read the leaves roll the dice shuffle the cards lay the runes write some poems and pray pray read the leaves roll the dice shuffle the cards lay the runes write some poems and pray read the leaves roll the dice shuffle the cards lay the runes write some poems and pray read the leaves roll the dice shuffle the cards lay the runes write some poems and pray read the leaves roll the dice shuffle the cards lay the runes write some poems and pray the odds

         read the leaves
         roll the dice
         shuffle the cards
         lay the runes
         write some poems
         and pray pray pray

TYRONE WILLIAMS

Constellation

A single strand of hair, black or brown for the eyes going bad,
delicately balanced on the dowel in the shower. . .

. . .the intermittent shelling of Gorzade. . .

Capsized in the center lane of I-70, a rowboat surprised us,
hungover, straining to the right as the wheel, spinning to the
left. . .

4200 dead at Manassas is not exhilirating for children capable of
killing several times that number at Circle Vision 360.

A single strand of hair, Julio Tavalaro, precariously balanced on a
towel holder, a fiber of immobilized terror, save the eyes, a world
of sighs, screams, whispers, a draft through an open window at
Goldwater Hospital. . .

I too am the chosen one, saith Judas.

Fort, da, smokes, empty glasses, a long-playing record mindlessly
spinning under a raised needle, stilletos, hiphuggers, Victoria's
Secrets, afire on the balcony, ditto for the bawled vows, the fresh
slate, the missing ingredient, "I'm going to the store," black money,
chasing the dragon, I'll Be Back. . .
What holds to the heel overcomes the head, so saith Esau, dreaming of
Achilles.

In the coliseum the orange lion lopes, pounces, leaps, plunges, into
the net to the whoops, the epithets, African American fruit, rack of
lamb, the lion from the pit, circles and circles of white
devils, of the world. . .

. . .or a single black tongue sings to a sea foaming at the mouth. . .

A strand of hair, Ho Dung, loss of limb, loss of sight, the Americans
still winning the conflict, teetering upon heaving bowels, a southpaw
clawing back up the Ho Chinh Minh Trail. . .

. . .a haunted palace "that literally exists, as T. exists, or E.,
or M.," tilting toward the fathers who are not parents. . .

"We do our own work" in fractious Orania, a high-wire act. . .

Nat Turner boards the 5:33 L.I.R.R. but an angel survives, slithers
on its belly into the temple at Hebron. . .

History as the invention of Wandering Jews, Brer Rabbits, draft
dodgers, mere recruits, mercenaries. . .

. . .or a little boy completely wrapped in Saran Wrap but for a single crooked
probe. . .

Or a single strand of hair, an "invisible filament running through
the undergrowth to a striker pin, a pencil-thin fuse," the alphabet
of aphasia, lost but for a single vowel, the one that never begins or
ends. . .

The gnarled remains of stump pain, the war of attrition which never
ends insinuates itself along ". . .the roads. . .the woodland paths. . .
the paddy fields. . .approaches to bridges. . .the side of dikes. . ."

Exponential mothers

Jose Chavez, at the end of the American Dream, drifts back and forth,
San Diego, Tijuana. . .

An installation of grieving mothers, a terra cotta alphabet, discrete
gestures among the commons. . .

Card

"The CEO Of Comedy . . . 'Hiya, fellas' . . . Bob Hope, Inc:
U.S.N.S. Bob Hope, Spirit of Bob Hope, G.I. Bob, Hope
Memorial Bridge, Bob Hope High School, Bob Hope Street, the Bob Hope
Chrysler Detroit Golf Classic, Bob Hope Theatre, the Bob Hope
Ferry, the Bob Hope rose, the Bob Hope Steer, Bobby Hope, Ben Hope,

Bill Hope. . .Lester Hope . . .Leslie Townes Hope. . ." discombobulated
status qua "ad lib" qua "standup"—"or a cheap imitation"
of a machine—a formula for comedy—breadth, not depth—
a stripmall of one-liners and gags, a search engine called Yucks
.com. Man walks into a bar. Man walks his wife—leash, please. Man

walks into a telephone booth. Man, that hurts. Man stops and walks
into a telephone booth that has no telephone. It was
b.y.o.p. Man walks—cave drawling at 11:00 P.M.
S.—man walks, no, runs. Man walks into a phone booth as a man,
leaves as a superman. Hope dressed up in another caper.

"Dispell'd"

after Walt Whitman's "Twilight"

Hereafter the so-called, remains no longer subject to the law of contraction and expansion intrinsic to dialectical materialism, no longer cohering in a "name" or a "body of work," no longer ideally irruptive ("anachronistic") or pandemic ("universal"), no longer—period,

however periodic, "Future/food. . .," bread for the tongue, trail through the underbrush, almost as if the "man" taking in was not the "man" taken in, the backtracking pioneer and all that double/shuttle thinking. . .

>On June 4, 1892 buckturing@earthlink.com wrote:
Is the that-called this?

>On August 4, 1892 wltpplsd@aol.com wrote:
Can "loss" as a sensation or principle exist before the "idea" of life?

"If the 'old artificer' is not the end of artificial intelligence, does it make any sense to speak of 'end' or 'ends'?"

". . .a prejudice. . .Perhaps. . ."

P: When the mouth, tongue, and related apparatus evolve into absolute or near oblivion—hair, nails, etc. notwithstanding—will the name assume the form of a "sense" (assuming the aforementioned—plural or singular—survive the machinery of vocalization)—touch-just-so, see-such-and-such, etc.?

S: In any case, will the name always be the synonym of a suffix, always esque, ist, ian et al? In short, is the name possible before "outside" iteration? Does the answer—yes and no—point elsewhere?

No one, and I mean *no* one, calls me out of my name and gets away with it, you understand, you hear what I'm saying, you read me, I will *kill* me some motherfucker, don't you *ever* call me, I mean *never* unless I tell you to, you got that? Huh? HUH??!!

:I'm_____
:Hi. I'm_____
:A start, if only.
:And yet we thought it important enough to begin with introductions, aka names, as though they were shell-gifts, hollowed-out presents in which we might hear one another's blood.
:There exists a logic whereby we'd merely divulge information according to the complex parameters of human intimacy and then, and only then, give names.
:As statement, as if in a court of law, as if the moment of giving, there was assertion.
:Violence, then, still. And always, I suppose.
:Perhaps start again?
:Impossible. It's all out, there.

And

    and

       and/then:

                     dislocation

           denames
             (almost)

       —or, momentarily—

(that is, before

  post-i e

El Negro

Here everyone—
             (in) or "in"—
                    is It—
          another name for "the"—
          or, decrossed, "-he"—
          delimbo-ed
      earthward,
first, at last, re-
             mains re
     stored re-
matriated
          to, by, the
motherland, her
           half-raised,
                half-made
           fist, dethumbed
        down to *all fours*
                    (do dodododo) lashed on,
   (da dadadadada) reined in, in
order to show,
            later, place—
Africa—as if
          borne-reborne-
              across-The-Big-Sea
                       (aka
            psuedo-warp
        psuedo-woof
is be
     diminished return
             delimited statute
     uncorrected proof.

Study of a Negro Head

This recalls a future "those_____. . ."
future *then*, future unannounced
however called for
                    Indefinite
(forced march? ticker tape? Brownian?)
hand-made, -maiden
drawing of my face in 1528

Briefly, a sketch

                    An hoped-for
enlightened antelope for
                    prides (going after)
An afeared scatting Pops-cum-Gus Hello Dolly/Chase
the wee slaveholder with legs
                    (a runner never running
out of the frame)

                    A drawn out
in cahoots with arresting (Big, White, etc.) houses

If Mime Then Music. . .

Pewed—half-staffed swastikas—
[organ voluntary]
Gregorian crescendoes,
belled by. Mini-stations
police the lamb fashioned out of gold.
[caroled organ] Adam
lay ybounden. Maiden, she makeless
[matchless], gentle. Better
Than the whole lot of them.
E'en so [organ responsary], quickly,
veni veni

Cold Calls

1 The spatial/temporal lacuna insures the possibility of temporary disruption—or permanent abortion—of service, insures only the probability of successful enunciation, its own passing over. Cf. Paul Laurence Dunbar as an example of such disruption, failure, breakdown: "My voice falls dead a foot from mine old lips/And but its ghost doth reach that vessel/passing, passing."[1]

2 God don't play that, so radio ratio—slippage: ebonics to tinkling the ivories, Eagle Nebula < M16, ice cream cones crowned with cherries, in short, EGGS, EGGS, EGGS . . . "In contrast, stars forming in more isolated circumstances presumably can continue to gather materials from surrounding gas clouds until their mature stellar dynamics halt their growth."[2]

3 Foreign respondent—"How White American"—Amy Biehl—
"'Sister'"—chased across a street— "Died in a Township"—after her
car was stopped—"one settler"—by a crowd of youths—"one bullet"—
tripped—"I am not able to properly articulate any political ideology or
motivation for my conduct"—fell—"South America is free today because
of the bloodshed."3

4 Essay in a bottle cast out to sea, or placed in a jar on a hill in Tennes-
see, Penelope, weaving and unweaving, Scheherazade's thousand-plus
deferments, time-lapsed Grecian Urn, bulk mailings, extensions of
credit lines, free-market economies: manifold apocrypha: hope a
project beyond approximate futures, Godot in which the thrown, not
yet thrown back, esse.

5 In the salad bowl of the museum, the Blonde Negress, a vigilant anachronism, deserts her post and joins her fellow patrons, a line refraining (in) the head she calls her body: "Lo, I am black but I am comely too." Among the periods, she attempts rememory: Is "but" conjunctive? Disjunctive? Her?[4]

6 Not *de gustibus* but homegoing, via Heaven's Gate (< Hale-Bopp)—
or another via: "Wherefore do we pray/Is not the God of the fathers
dead?"[5] Or yet still a third via: "teeth or trees or lemons piled on a
step."[6] Or yet still: two men sitting at a bar. One turns to the other:
"Aren't you *the* Artie Shaw?" The other retorts: "No, I'm the other
one."[7] Despite the end of identical actions at a distance (< Schrodinger's
equation), pursuit converts us: ancestors of our hope, the via, the
nectar.

7 from someone who, no longer there, abandoned headset swinging
back and forth, fruit laced with strange, charm, top, and bottom—not
vocabularized but ventriloquized—in an upright glass coffin rhyming
with the "rough-hewn tribute in wood" to an anonymous African
American rider, not "divinity alive in stone" aka "William Tecumseh
Sherman at Fifth Ave. and 60th Street in Birmingham, Ala." An anti-
Trojan, virus astride.[8]

8 Inaudible howl, "foo seee like lee,"[9] the diving chrysalis[10]—hell with a little heaven in it[11]—and should it surface, should it find its way back home, should its first night back on earth not be its last.

9 Ambivalence of double cadence: an extra nail, or the anvil then the claw.

10 "Neither there nor there/ Almost here/ a little nearer to the stars/ strangers to the left and right/ pages turned, still to be turned,/ still there, never to be mine/ and here comes a smile/ which never arrives—/ 'Can I get you something?'/ 'Food/ For future years.'"[12]

11 "All this in the hands of children, eyes already set/ on a land we never can visit—it isn't there yet—"[13]

12 The "apron of leaves," the pieces of silver—what human, having embodied God as shame and guilt, would not be disappointed that only the same could disembody him?[14]

13 The New Grammar: Neo-Babel: "Trucks, limousines and pickups . . . smashed to pieces." Crashing into a skyscraper, a Boeing jet "disgorged its sinful passengers," "bodies spilling across the road into 'The Peaceful View' cemetery"—paradigm of grammar and Babel—from which their spirits "floated upwards a glowing image of Jesus high in the clouds."[15]

14 "A door ajar/ bereft of building/ remains unapproachable/ and
mesmerizing." Tenor ISO vehicle. Rapture preferred but not essential.
Will settle for oblique transport.

15 you@notyetorever.com v .net v .org v .edu v

END NOTES

1. Paul Laurence Dunbar, "Ships That Pass In The Night," *The Complete Poems of Paul Laurence Dunbar* (Hakim's Publications, 210 South 52nd Street, Philadelphia, PA 19139), p. 64.

2. *The New York Times,* 11/3/95 and 11/30/95, Science Sections.

3. *The New York Times,* 8/27/93 and 7/9/97.

4. Lewis Alexander, "The Dark Brother," *Caroling Dusk,* edited and with a foreword by Countee Cullen (Citadel Press, 1993; orig. Harpers & Brothers, 1927), p. 124.

5. W.E.B. DuBois, "A Litany of Atlanta," *Caroling Dusk*, p. 27.

6. Amiri Baraka, "Black Art," *Transbluesency: Selected Poems 1961-1995,* edited by Paul Vangelisti (Marsilio Publishers, New York: 1995), p. 142.

7. *The New York Times,* 8/19/94.

8. Claude McKay, "Russian Cathedral," *Caroling Dusk*, p. 88; Judith Shea's "The Other Monument," as reported in *The New York Times,* 8/24/95.

9. Julia Tavalaro and Richard Tayson, *Look Up For Yes* (Kodansha International, 1997), p. 12.

10. Jean Dominique Bauby, *The Diving Bell And The Butterfly*, trans. by Jeremy Leggatt (Alfred A. Knopf, 1997).

11. George MacDonald: "There is no heaven with a little hell in it." Circa 1886.

12. William Wordsworth, "Tintern Abbey," in *English Romantic Writers,* edited by David Perkins (Harcourt Brace Jovanovich, Inc., 1967), p. 210.

13. Miller Williams, "Of History and Hope," *The Ways We Touch* (University of Illinois Press, 1997).

14. Elaine Scarry, *The Body In Pain* (Oxford University Press, 1985), p. 360, footnote 23.

15. "The Coming Rapture," painting by an unknown artist, in Jeremy Marre and Hannah Charlton, *Beats Of The Heart: Popular Music Of The World* (Pantheon Books, 1985), p. 57.

from Bar Code

3. Category

black noir–
                circa 1991, during
Black History Year: bitstorms: unbridled unos,
nadas, plus reparations at cost, calibrated
to the precedents of tort law, and another
thing–you wouldn't understand–is this, moreover,
displacement of Once Upon A Time by N The Hood–
                                                (Wink)

from Bar Code

9. Quiet Zone

Too "inside" the wrong side of the camera,
Still, a table near the kitchen, a long spoon,
give the finger to us to

PRESS THE SPACE BAR

room to let, begin and end,
pro patria mori, like the dutiful,
prodigal son, divided in two, brothers
wrestling to a draw which resembles the peace
passed understanding . . .

PRESS RETURN OR ENTER

and separation
means sin, means grace: back to bad, forward to good,
hair, schools, neighborhoods . . .

WINDOWS ~~BE~~/IS SHUTTING DOWN

RONALDO V. WILSON

On the C Train the Black Object Ponders Amuzati's Family Eaten in the Congo

Cut the adults. Huck-um dun the chest,
the deceased lumps.

In the story of the edible blacks, hacked and splayed on lattice,
how am I to finish the dishes

with all this dining
in the fields of my instance?

Unremit by browned lung, blisters are blisters, dry by sun,
bucks into bits.

Lattice, works: business is business after all,
but did the Black-Back-Fat deserve its end like the tic I popped?

Sure, if the tic could, it would visa out of grip.
But, sorry, the sweet, sweet spleens!

In the magazine, NYT, a teeny pink baby
teeters on the crease of a big palm, cream and light:

Daddy! I am so hungry for some Pyg.

Such hunger, subwayed, the crust on the bittle lack's head
skin, where hair, a spiral spurns beneath flesh.

Ring worm, rung'un, crunk of nap. Mother to baby: *Shut up!*
Don't touch me, Suckcandysuckit. *C'mon now chile'.*

51. Lucy, Her River and Sky

The current let me swim up against the waterfall, until the edge of it swept me out over the rocks into an eddy, where I shut my eyes.

I did not imagine leeches sticking to my body. In fact, I thought of the sun, a bright spot in the gray field I snapped a shot of before I left home.

I am waiting, here, at the edge of the river's shore, staring from under my own blood, my eyes shut until the red reels behind them.

A sea sheen shoots across the sky, and I vacate to clear across space.
I am useless.

I am less than the rock I am laying on, less than moss, green and unseen
    but I feel flat and secure after falling in its rush.

Out of the river, up on a rock, the forest is invisible, because I am lost in the
    middle of it. I unwind to nothing.

Sometimes, my body floats out of control, but here on a ledge, where the
    water
pushes out over me into more water, I can breathe.

There is no one to see this. There is none, but an edge of rock. I am here,
un-named, un-object, lying.

In the air, I look up at a line between what I see–my sky–and what I can't,
the inside of my eyelids lit with an orange I've not seen this bright.

Staring into it on my back, floating in the current, I look up into what my
    sight,
splits. Here: who would say I am?

I am not like the water, flat and brown. I am not liquid, fish, or to be read as
anything but human.

My fat back keeps me surfaced, unturned over. I float. My arms spread out to keep me still. I know there is a black on the shore, his gut, earthed in by muscle.

Unmarked. Am I white, here, out at the edge of flow?
My body lost and no-one to call me: anything.

The Black Object's Elasticity

It's not as though I felt my body. It's not like I will ever return. In a room, where midnight blue coats the wall, and a black light is bolted to the ceiling, a shirt glows white. A horizon of two bulbs cut the room to a yellow painted galaxy in the corner. Not from daylight, or sunrise or a window, I escape fluorescence.

"Fuck You!" "Enjoy your hike back to New York!" "I'm confused." "I'm not even sure why I'm doing this." Answering machines can take such, but how to take being called an idiot by an illiterate and to be recalled by that name until three in the morning by this stranger, an alcoholic, a truck driver, who eats steak and beans.

There are ways to evade abuse I surmise, some of which have to do with finding a replica of your abuser. One face becomes another face. The red eyes of a lover whose wife is sick, who longs for she-males, who has left his ten acre house and lives in a beige box in a trailer park are replaceable by the right tuft of beard.

I will always remember that flash of his body, where the hips slipped away to a redness peeling off the buttock, the rotted nail in the toe, or the teddy bear in the bed the therapist wanted him to cuddle. What I want is to extend from one decay to another – beer breath to yellow teeth to his eyes sunk to hurt.

I feel like a disembodied car part: a pop-up headlight's internal arm that breaks then stabs the radiator, dooming the engine. I know the difference between the engine's injury and the knife in the dish rack, my running as clear as the distance between the moon, running at night, and the treadmill, running in one place.

CONTRIBUTORS

Will Alexander, long time Los Angeles resident, has most recently published *Compression & Purity, On the Substance of Disorder, Diary as Sin, Inside the Earthquake Palace, Mirach Speaks to His Grammatical Transparents, Singing in the Magnetic Hoofbeat, The Brimstone Boat, Aboriginal Salt: Early Divinations, Towards the Primeval Lightning Field,* and *Kaleidoscopic Omniscience.* He is the recipient of a 2007 PEN Oakland National Book Award for the novel *Sunrise In Armageddon,* as well as a 2013 American Book Award for the book of essays *Singing In Magnetic Hoofbeat.*

Ron Allen, a Detroit native, was a playwright as well as a poet. He first experienced life outside the United States when cooking for U.S. troops in the jungles of Viet Nam. To make sense of all he'd seen, felt and heard, as a cook and as a ground troop, Ron resumed writing poetry upon his return home. A reading series cofounded by Allen, Horizons in Poetry, stands with Dudley Randall's Broadside Press as a center for new and seasoned poets. His volumes of poetry include *I Want My Body Back, Neon Jawbone Riot* and *The Unborn Muse of Shadows.* Allen's theatrical works include *Eye Mouth Graffiti Body Shop, Relative Energy Sack Theory Museum, Aboriginal Treatment Center* and *Entertainer Zero Machine.* His final autobiographical statement to the editors of this volume was, "I search the weightlessness of language / to create metaphor and hyper-foliage / in my word laboratory weightless language."

T. J. Anderson III has an MFA from the University of Michigan and a PhD from Binghamton University. A former Fulbright Scholar at Cairo University, he is the author of *Notes to Make the Sound Come Right: Four Innovators of Jazz Poetry* (University of Arkansas Press), *River to Cross* (Backwaters Press), *Cairo Workbook* (Willow Books), the Spoken-Word CD, *Blood Octave*

(Flat Five Recordings), and the chapbook *At Last Round Up* (lift books). He teaches courses in jazz literature, African American literature, poetry and performance, and creative writing at Hollins University.

Tisa Bryant is the author of *Tzimmes, Unexplained Presence,* and *[the curator]*. She has appeared in many journals, including *Mixed Blood, Mandorla, Universal Remote,* and *Evening Will Come.* She is the publisher and coeditor of *The Encyclopedia Project*, and teaches at California Institute of the Arts.

Pia Deas holds a masters degree from Temple University and a PhD from Penn State University. She curated an exhibit titled "Changing the Joke/ Slipping the Yoke: Humor in African American Fiction." She is currently an assistant professor at Lincoln University.

C.S. Giscombe is a professor in the Department of English at the University of California, Berkeley. His many volumes of poetry include *Postcards, Here, At Large, Giscome Road,* and *Prairie Style.* He is also the author of the prose work *Into and Out of Dislocation.*

Renee Gladman is a writer and visual artist living in Providence, Rhode Island. The works included in this anthology are culled from the following previously published work: *Not Right Now* (Second Story Books, 1999), *Juice* (Kelsey St. Press, 2000), and *The Activist* (Krupskaya, 2003). More recent work includes the Ravicka novels, published by Dorothy Publishing Project.

Duriel E. Harris is the cofounder of the Black Took Collective and Editor of *Obsidian: Literature & Arts in the African Diaspora.* She is the author of *Drag, Amnesiac: Poems,* and *Speleology* (video). Nominated for the Pushcart Prize, recent writing appears in *Fifth Wednesday* and *Kweli* as well as *The Force of What's Possible* and *The &Now Awards 3.* A poet, performance artist, and scholar, Harris is a member of Douglas Ewart & Inventions creative music ensemble and Call & Response—a dynamic of Black women in performance. Current projects include the sound compilation "Black Magic" and *Thingification*—a one-woman show.

Harmony Holiday has studied and taught dance and writing at Columbia University. Her first book is *Negro League Baseball.*

Erica Hunt is a poet and essayist. She is the author of *Local History, ARCADE, Piece Logic,* and *Time Slips.* Her work has appeared in *Poetics Journal, BOMB,*

Iowa Review, Tripwire, In the American Tree, The Politics of Poetic Form, and *Moving Borders: Three Decades of Innovative Writing by Women,* among other venues. She lives in New York City.

Kim D. Hunter is a lifelong Detroiter employed in media relations for nonprofits. He has served as poet-in-residence in several Detroit public schools through the IndieOut Literary Arts Program. He codirects the ten-year-old Woodward Line Poetry Series. His work appears in *Rainbow Darkness, Abandon Automobile Triage, Hipology, Metro Times, Dispatch Detroit,* and *Graffiti Rag.* He has published two collections of poetry, *borne on slow knives* and *edge of the time zone.* He received a Kresge Literary Arts Fellowship in 2012 for short fiction.

Geoffrey Jacques is a poet and critic currently living in California. His poetry volumes are *Hunger and Other Poems, Suspended Knowledge,* and *Just for a Thrill.* His critical study, *A Change in the Weather: Modernist Imagination, African American Imaginary,* was published by the University of Massachusetts Press.

Douglas Kearney is a poet, performer, librettist, and the author of *Fear, Some, The Black Automaton,* and *Patter.* His honors include a Whiting Writers Award. He currently teaches at California Institute of the Arts.

John Keene, a faculty member at Rutgers University–Newark, is the author of *Annotations, Seismosis,* and *Counternarratives,* and translator of Brazilian author Hilda Hilst's *Letters from a Seducer.* His honors include a Whiting Foundation Award.

Nathaniel Mackey won the National Book Award for his volume *Splay Anthem.* His other books of poetry include *Eroding Witness, Four for Trane, Septet for the End of Time, Outlantish, Four for Glenn, School of Udhra, Whatsaid Serif,* and *Nod House.* He is also the author of a serial work of fiction titled *From a Broken Bottle Traces of Perfume Still Emanate,* of which five volumes have been published to date. He was the 2015 winner of the Bollingen Prize.

Dawn Lundy Martin completed a PhD in English literature at the University of Massachusetts in Amherst, and now teaches at the University of Pittsburgh. She is the author of *The Morning Hour,* a collection of poems that was selected in 2003 by C. D. Wright for the Poetry Society of America's

National Chapbook Fellowship. In 2002 and 2006, Martin was awarded a Massachusetts Cultural Council Artists Grant for Poetry and has published poems in several journals including, most recently, *Callaloo, nocturnes (re) view of the literary arts* and *Encyclopedia*. Martin is also a founding member of the Black Took Collective, a group of experimental black poets. She is co-editor of the collection of essays, *The Fire This Time: Young Activists and the New Feminism* (Anchor Books, 2004), and a cofounder of the only national young feminist organization in the United States, the Third Wave Foundation in New York. Her recent books are *A Gathering of Matter/A Matter of Gathering* and *Life in a Box is a Pretty Life*.

Mark McMorris, a professor at Georgetown University, is the author of *The Black Reeds, The Blaze of the Poui, Moth-Wings, The Café at Light, Palinurus Suite, Figure for a Hypothesis, Entrepôt*, and other works.

Tracie Morris, a graduate of Hunter College and New York University, is currently on the faculty of the Pratt Institute. Her books include *Intermission, TDJ: To Do with John*, and *Rhyme Scheme*. She is also developing two audio projects: *The Tracie Morris Band* and *sharpmorris*, a collaboration with composer Elliott Sharp.

Fred Moten is a professor at the University of California, Riverside. His first critical volume is *In the Break: The Aesthetics of the Black Radical Tradition*. Moten's books of poetry include *B Jenkins, Arkansas, Hughson's Tavern, The Feel Trio*, and *The Little Edges*. With Stefano Harney he is the coauthor of *The Undercommons: Fugitive Planning and Black Study*.

Harryette Mullen is a recipient of the Jackson Poetry Award and the Stephen Henderson Award. Among her books are *Tree Tall Woman, Trimings, S*PeRM**K*T, Muse & Drudge, Sleeping with the Dictionary, Recyclopedia*, and *Urban Tumbleweed: Notes from a Tanka Diary*. She is a professor of English at the University of California, Los Angeles.

Mendi Lewis Obadike won the Naomi Long Madgett Award for her first collection of poetry, *Armor and Flesh*. A multimedia artist, she has received commissions from the Whitney Museum, Electronic Arts Intermix, and the New York African Film Festival. A frequent collaborator with her husband, composer and performance artist Keith Obadike, she wrote the libretto for the opera *The Sour Thunder*.

G. E. Patterson is the author of *Tug* and *To and From*. After studying at Princeton and Stanford, he settled in Saint Paul, Minnesota, teaching at Metropolitan State University.

Julie Ezelle Patton is a conceptual artist and community activist based out of New York City for thirty years, but with attachments to Cleveland. She is the author of *Teething on Type* and *BS*. A recipient of the first annual New York City Arts in Education Award for Sustained Achievement, she has taught and developed curricula for museums, colleges, and learning initiatives. She has collaborated with filmmakers Henry Hills and Euphrosene Bloom and dancers Daria Failn and Sally Silver.

Claudia Rankine is the author of the poetry collections *Citizen, Don't Let Me Be Lonely, The End of the Alphabet,* and *Plot* and of the plays *Provenance of Beauty: A South Bronx Travelogue* and *Existing Conditions*, coauthored with Casey Llewellyn. Rankine is the coeditor of *American Women Poets in the Twenty-First Century* series with Wesleyan University Press. A recipient of fellowships from the Academy of American Poets and the National Endowment for the Arts, she teaches at Pomona College.

Deborah Richards was born in London. She has work published in *nocturnes (re)view of the literary arts, XCP: Cross-Cultural Poetics, Encyclopedia Vol. 1* and *Callaloo*. She is the author of the chapbook, *parable* (Leroy Press 2002) and a collection of poems *Last One Out* (subpress 2003). She is currently working on *The Book of Anthony* and collating refugee students' writing.

Evie Shockley is the author of two books of poetry—*the new black* (Wesleyan, 2011), winner of the 2012 Hurston/Wright Legacy Award, and *a half-red sea* (Carolina Wren, 2006)—and the critical study *Renegade Poetics: Black Aesthetics and Formal Innovation in African American Poetry* (Iowa, 2011). She currently serves as creative writing editor for *Feminist Studies* and teaches African American literature and creative writing at Rutgers University–New Brunswick.

giovanni singleton won the California Book Award for her first volume of poetry, *Ascension*. She received an MFA from the New College of California. She is the founding editor and publisher of the journal *nocturnes (re)view of the literary arts*. Her work has appeared in such publications as *Five Fingers Review, Fence, Aufgabe, Proliferation, Chain,* and *Callaloo*.

Tyrone Williams, a faculty member at Xavier University, is the author of *c.c., Adventures of Pi, Howell, On Spec, Convalescence,* and *The Hero Project of the Century.*

Ronaldo V. Wilson's poetry recently appears in *Blithe House Quarterly, Callaloo, Corpus 4, Fence, Harvard Review, nocturnes (re)view of the literary arts,* and *The Encyclopedia Project.* He is a cofounder of the Black Took Collective and has held residencies at the Fine Arts Work Center in Provincetown, The Vermont Studio Center, Yaddo, and Djerassi. His books include *Poems of the Black Object* and *Narrative of the Life of the Brown Boy and the White Man,* and he is a winner of the Cave Canem Poetry Prize.